District Gazetteers of India Series 154

MADRAS DISTRICT GAZETTEERS

STATISTICAL APPENDIX

FOR

TINNEVELLY

District Gazetteers of India Series 154

MADRAS DISTRICT GAZETTEERS

STATISTICAL APPENDIX

FOR

TINNEVELLY

23 VOLUMES (IN 25 BINDINGS)

(VOL. 21st)

GYAN

Published by

Gyan Publishing House
5, Ansari Road
Daryaganj, New Delhi-110002
Phone: 011-47034999, 9811692060
E-mail: books@gyanbooks.com

Distribution Network
gyanbooks.com
India, USA, Canada, UK, Australia, France

ISBN: 978-93-6208-562-7 (Set) 23 Volumes (In 25 Bindings)
978-81-212-5841-8 (PB)

First Published, 1915

2nd Impression 2024

Printed at: Gyan Press, Delhi.

MADRAS DISTRICT GAZETTEERS (Vol. 21st)

LIST OF VOLUMES

S. NO.	ISBN NO.	VOLUME	TITLE	AUTHOR	PRICE	PAGES
			ASSAM DISTRICT GAZETTEERS			
1	9788121285926	1st	Cachar	B. C. Allen	600	300
2	9788121285919	2nd	Sylhet	B. C. Allen	750	378
3	9788121285902	3rd	Goalpara	B. C. Allen	400	203
4	9788121285896	4th	Kamrup	B. C. Allen	675	344
5	9788121285889	5th	Darrang	B. C. Allen	725	364
6	9788121285872	6th	Nowgong	B. C. Allen	560	280
7	9788121285865	7th	Sibsagar	B. C. Allen	675	343
8	9788121285858	8th	Lakhimpur	B. C. Allen	690	347
9	9788121285841	9th	Naga Hills and Manipur	B. C. Allen	580	294
10	9788121285834	10th	The Khasi And Jaintia Hills, The Garo Hills And The Lushai Hills	B. C. Allen	675	363
11	9788121285827	11th	The Sadiya and Balipara Frontier Tract	B. C. Allen	375	190
			BENGAL DISTRICT GAZETTEERS			
12	9788121218672	1st	Angul	L. S. S. O'Malley	340	168
13	9788121259637	2nd	Bakarganj	J. C. JACK	970	194
14	9788121218696	3rd	Balasore	L. S. S. O'Malley	450	228
15	9788121259590	4th	Bankura	L. S. S. O'Malley	1000	199
16	9788121218375	5th	Bhagalpur	J. Byrne	390	194
17	9788121218290	6th	Birbhum	L. S. S. O'Malley	300	150
18	9788121259651	7th	Eastern Bengal and Assam - Bogra	J. N. Gupta	940	188
19	9788121218351	8th	Burdwan	J. C. K. Peterson	450	227
20	9788121259538	9th	Calcutta District Gazetteer - Statistics, 1901 - 02		340	68
21	9788121218313	10th	Champaran	L. S. S. O'Malley	410	205
22	9788121259613	11th	Eastern Bengal District Gazetters - Chittagong	L. S. S. O'Malley	1080	216
23	9788121259552	12th	Chota Nagpur Tributary		130	26
24	9788121259415	13th	The Cooch Behar Gazette: Statistics		1460	292
25	9788121218412	14th	Cuttack	L. S. S. O'Malley	490	248
26	9788121261357	15th	Eastern Bengal District Gazetteers Dacca	B. C. Allen	400	207
27	9788121218436	16th	Darbhanga	L. S. S. O'Malley	360	180
28	9789362089335	17th	Darjeeling	L. S. S. O'Malley	500	248
29	9788121259453	18th	Eastern Bengal District Gazetteers - Dinajpur	F. W. Strong	890	178
30	9788121259392	19th	Faridpur	L. S. S. O'Malley	700	140
31	9788121218474	20th	Gaya	L. S. S. O'Malley	540	270
32	9788121214032	21st	Bihar and Orissa District Gazetteer: Hazaribagh	E. Lister	715	234
33	9788121218337	22nd	Hooghly	L. S. S. O'Malley	680	340
34	9788121218191	23rd	Bengal District Gazetteer Howrah	L. S. S. O'Malley	390	199
35	9788121259293	24th	Eastern Bengal and Assam - Jalpaiguri	John F. Gruning	890	178
36	9788121259279	25th	Jessore	L. S. S. O'Malley	960	192
37	9788121259231	26th	Khulna	L. S. S. O'Malley	1100	220
38	9788121259217	27th	Malda	G. E. Lambourn	670	134
39	9788121267854	28th	Manbhum	H. Coupland	600	313
40	9788121218498	29th	Midnapore	L. S. S. O'Malley	500	252
41	9788121218597	30th	Monghyr	L. S. S. O'Malley	560	280
42	9788121259156	31st	Murshidabad	L. S. S. O'Malley	1250	250
43	9788121259576	32nd	Bengal District Gazetteers - Muzaffarpur	L. S. S. O'Malley	940	188
44	9788121259132	33rd	Mymensingh	F. A. Sachse	960	192
45	9788121259118	34th	Nadia	J. H. E. Garrett	1070	214
46	9788121259095	35th	Eastern Bengal and Assam - Noakhali	J. E. Webster	580	115
47	9788121218450	36th	Feudatory States of Orissa	L. E. B. Cobdenramsay	790	395
48	9788121259071	37th	Pabna	L. S. S. O'Malley	710	142
49	9788121218511	38th	Palamau	L. S. S. O'Malley	380	190
50	9788121218634	39th	Patna	L. S. S. O'Malley	500	250
51	9788121218535	40th	Puri	L. S. S. O'Malley	650	328
52	9788121218757	41st	Purnea	L. S. S. O'Malley	440	220
53	9788121258937	42nd	Rajshahi	L. S. S. O'Malley	1080	216
54	9788121256681	43rd	Bihar and Orissa District Gazetteers: Ranchi	M. G. Hallett	1350	278
55	9788121258913	44th	Eastern Bengal and assam - Rangpur	J. A. Vas	890	178
56	9788121218559	45th	Sambalpur	L. S. S. O'Malley	480	242
57	9788121214056	46th	Santal Parganas	L. S. S. O'Malley	940	308
58	9788121218610	47th	Saran	L. S. S. O'Malley	380	190
59	9788121218658	48th	Shahabad	L. S. S. O'Malley	380	190
60	9788121256704	49th	The Gazetteer of Sikhim	H. H. Risley	960	481
61	9788121218573	50th	Singhbhum, Saraikela And Kharsawan	L. S. S. O'Malley	560	280
62	9788121259439	51st	Eastern Bengal District Gazetteers - Tippera	J. E. Webster	730	146
63	9788121259033	52nd	24 Parganas	L. S. S. O'Malley	1420	284

S. NO.	ISBN NO.	VOLUME	TITLE	AUTHOR	PRICE	PAGES
			CENTRAL PROVINCES DISTRICT GAZETTEERS			
64	9789362081728	1st, Vol. A	Akola (Descriptive)	A. E. Nelson, C. Brown	870	436
65	9789362085481	2nd, Vol. A	Amraoti (Descriptive)	S. V. Fitzgerald, A. E. Nelson	1050	524
66	9789362089267	3rd,Vol. A	Balaghat (Descriptive)	R. V. RUSSELL	430	216
67	9789362083494	4th, Vol. A	Betul (Descriptive)	R. V. RUSSELL	610	306
68	9789362085146	5th, Vol. A	Bhandara (Descriptive)	R. V. RUSSELL	580	292
69	9789362088390	6th, Vol. A	Bilaspur (Descriptive)	R. V. RUSSELL	870	434
70	9789362086044	7th, Vol. A	Buldana (Descriptive)	A. E. Nelson	1090	543
71	9789362089014	8th, Vol. B	Chanda (Descriptive)	R. V. RUSSELL	470	234
72	9789362086938	9th	Chhattisgarch Feudatory State	E. A. De Brett	880	440
73	9789362082961	10th	Chhindwara (Descriptive)	R. V. RUSSELL	550	274
74	9789362089342	11th, Vol. A & B	Damoh (Descriptive and Statistical Tables 1891-1901)	R. V. RUSSELL	830	414
75	9789362081230	12th, Vol. A	Durg (Descriptive)	A. E. Nelson	460	232
76	9789362086037	13th, Vol. A	Hoshangabad (Descriptive)	R. V. RUSSELL	860	430
77	9789362086792	14th, Vol. A	Jubbulpore (Descriptive)	A. E. Nelson	950	474
78	9789362089663	15th, Vol. A & B	Mandla (Descriptive and Statistical Tables 1891-1901)	R. V. RUSSELL	370	186
79	9789362086419	16th, Vol. A	Nagpur (Descriptive)	R. V. RUSSELL	790	394
80	9789362080646	17th, Vol. A	Narsinghpur (Descriptive)	R. V. RUSSELL	510	257
81	9789362084835	18th, Vol. A	Nimar (Descriptive)	R. V. RUSSELL	600	299
82	9789362087737	19th, Vol. A	Raipur (Descriptive)	A. E. Nelson	790	396
83	9789362080264	20th, Vol. A	Saugor (Descriptive)	R. V. RUSSELL	570	285
84	9789362081117	21st, Vol. A	Seoni (Descriptive)	R. V. RUSSELL	460	232
85	9789362084965	22nd, Vol. A	Wardha (Descriptive)	R. V. RUSSELL	600	302
86	9789362083401	23rd, Vol. A	Yeotmal (Descriptive)	R. V. RUSSELL	550	277
87	9789362080325	24th, Vol. I, Pt. I	Gwalior (Text and Tables)	R. V. RUSSELL	980	489
88	9789362087133	24th, Vol. I, Pt. II	Gwalior (Maps)	R. V. RUSSELL	400	198
89	9789362086341	24th, Vol. I, Pt. III	Gwalior (Village List)	R. V. RUSSELL	810	406
90	9789362085467	24th, Vol. I, Pt. IV	Gwalior (Photos)	R. V. RUSSELL	1400	698
91	9789362087393	25th, Vol. II	Indore (Text and Tables)	C. E. Luard	1050	524
92	9789362084422	26th, Vol. III	Bhopal (Text and Tables)	C. E. Luard	540	272
93	9789362086815	27th, Vol. IV	Rewah (Text and Tables)	C. E. Luard	500	250
94	9789362087584	28th, Vol. V, Pt. A	Western States - Malwa (Text)	C. E. Luard	1520	762
95	9789362087300	29th, Vol. VI, Pt. A	Eastern States - Bundelkhand (Text)	C. E. Luard	930	463
96	9789362082169	30th, Vol. VI, Pt. B	Eastern States - Bundelkhand (Tables)	C. E. Luard	830	417
			GAZETTEER OF THE BOMBAY PRESIDENCY:			
97	9788121283441	1st, Part I	History of Gujarat	Ed.: James M. Campbell	3220	644
98	9788121285582	1st, Part II	History of the Konkan Dakhan and Southern Maratha Country	Ed.: James M. Campbell	4200	840
99	9788121285568	2nd	Gujarat, Surat and Broach	Ed.: James M. Campbell	2990	598
100	9788121285544	3rd	Kaira and Panch Mahals	Ed.: James M. Campbell	1690	339
101	9788121285520	4th	Ahmedabad	Ed.: James M. Campbell	1860	372
102	9788121285506	5th	Cutch, Palanpur, and Mahi Kantha	Ed.: James M. Campbell	2390	478
103	9788121285483	6th	Rewa Kantha, Narukot, Cambay, and Surat States	Ed.: James M. Campbell	1450	290
104	9788121285469	7th	Baroda	Ed.: James M. Campbell	3260	652
105	9788121285445	8th	Kathiawar	Ed.: James M. Campbell	3790	758
106	9788121285421	9th, Part I	Gujarat Population - Hindus	Ed.: James M. Campbell	3170	636
107	9788121285407	9th, Part II	Gujarat Population - Musalmans and Parsis	Ed.: James M. Campbell	1520	304
108	9788121285384	10th	Ratnagiri and Savantvadi	Ed.: James M. Campbell	2500	501
109	9788121285360	11th	Kolaba and Janjira	Ed.: James M. Campbell	2550	513
110	9788121285346	12th	Khandesh	Ed.: James M. Campbell	3190	638
111	9788121285322	13th Part I	Thana	Ed.: James M. Campbell	2050	413
112	9788121285308	13th Part II	Thana	Ed.: James M. Campbell	1770	357
113	9788121285285	14th	Thana - Places of Interest	Ed.: James M. Campbell	3290	659
114	9788121285261	15th Part I	Kanara	Ed.: James M. Campbell	2340	348
115	9788121285247	15th Part II	Kanara	Ed.: James M. Campbell	1740	348
116	9788121285223	16th	Nasik	Ed.: James M. Campbell	3490	698
117	9788121285209	17th	Ahmadnagar	Ed.: James M. Campbell	3860	772
118	9788121285186	18th Part I	Poona	Ed.: James M. Campbell	2930	586
119	9788121285162	18th Part II	Poona	Ed.: James M. Campbell	2680	537
120	9788121285148	18th Part III	Poona	Ed.: James M. Campbell	2500	503
121	9788121285124	19th	Satara	Ed.: James M. Campbell	3450	692
122	9788121285100	20th	Sholapur	Ed.: James M. Campbell	2730	547
123	9788121285087	21st	Gazetteer of the Bomaby Presidency: Belgaum	Ed.: James M. Campbell	2570	514
124	9788121285063	22nd	Dharwar	Ed.: James M. Campbell	4200	841
125	9788121285049	23rd	Gazetteer of the Bombay Presidency:Bijapur	Ed.: James M. Campbell	3550	712
126	9788121285025	24th	Kolhapur	Ed.: James M. Campbell	2250	450

S. NO.	ISBN NO.	VOLUME	TITLE	AUTHOR	PRICE	PAGES
127	9788121285001	25th	Botany	Ed.: James M. Campbell	2040	408
128	9788121284981	26th, Part I	Materials Towards a Statistical Account of the Town and Island of Bombay - History	Ed.: James M. Campbell	2500	504
129	9788121284967	26th, Part II	Materials Towards a Statistical Account of the Town and Island of Bombay - Trade and Fortifications	Ed.: James M. Campbell	2690	538
130	9788121284943	26th, Part III	Materials Towards a Statistical Account of the Town And Island of Bombay - Administration	Ed.: James M. Campbell	2450	702
131	9788121284929	27th	General Index	Ed.:R. E. Enthoven	2190	428
			MADRAS DISTRICT GAZETTEERS			
132	9788121258814	1st	Anantapur	W. Francis	1140	227
133	9788121258555	2nd	Malabar	C. A Innes & F. B Evans	3010	602
134	9788121258791	3rd	Bellary	W. Francis	1890	377
135	9788121258777	4th	Statistical Appendix For Chingleput		280	56
136	9788121258753	5th	Coimbatore	K. N. Krishnaswami Ayyar	3420	628
137	9788121232814	6th	Madras District Gazetteers District Gazetteer Cuddapah	C. F. Brackenbury	1120	285
138	9788121258715	7th	Statistical Appendix For Ganjam		370	73
139	9788121256766	8th, Vol. 1st	Godavari District Gazetteer	F. R. Hemingway	650	320
140	9788121256803	8th, Vol. 2nd	Godavari District Gazetteer	F. R. Hemingway	160	83
141	9788121258678	9th	Statistical Appendix For Kistna		640	127
142	9788121258654	10th	Statistical Appendix For Kurnool		270	54
143	9788121258616	11th	Madura	W. Francis	1900	379
144	9788121258579	12th	Statistical Appendix For Madura		740	148
145	9788121258630	13th	The Nilgiris	W. Francis	2190	437
146	9788121234276	14th	Madras District Gazetteers Gazetteer Of The Nellore District Brought Upto 1938		1150	386
147	9788121258517	15th	North Arcot		590	118
148	9788121258494	16th, Vol. 1, Part I	Salem	F. J. Richards	1710	343
149	9788121258593	16th, Vol. 1, Part II	Salem	F. J. Richards	1800	360
150	9788121258456	17th	South Arcot	W. Francis	2400	480
151	9788121258470	18th	Statistical Appendix For South Canara		400	80
152	9788121258432	19th, Vol. 1st & 2nd	Tanjore: Main Volume and Statistical Appendix		2070	401
153	9788121258395	20th	Tinnevelly	H. R. Pate	2740	547
154	9788121258418	21st	Statistical Appendix For Tinnevelly		320	64
155	9788121258371	22nd, 1st & 2nd	Trichinopoly: Main Volume and Statistical Appendix	F. R. Hemingway	2440	487
156	9788121241953	23rd	Vizagapatam District Gazetteer	W. Francis	760	385
			PUNJAB DISTRICT GAZETTEERS			
157	9788121255943	1st	Ambala District 1883-84		620	124
158	9788121255967	2nd	Amritsar		1180	236
159	9788121255981	3rd	Delhi		1300	260
160	9788121256001	4th	Ferozepore		950	188
161	9788121256025	5th	Faridkot		350	70
162	9788121256049	6th	Gujranwala 1893-94		1270	254
163	9788121256063	7th	Gujrat	C. E. Luard	1140	228
164	9788121256087	8th	Gurdaspur 1891-92		1260	252
165	9788121256100	9th	Gurgaon 1883-4		1020	203
166	9788121256124	10th	Hazara	H. D. Watson	2290	458
167	9788121256148	11th	Hissar district and Lohar State		1840	367
168	9788121256162	12th	Hoshiarpur		1420	283
169	9788121256186	13th	Jhang		1070	213
170	9788121256209	14th	Jhelam		1010	202
171	9788121256223	15th	Jalandhar District 1883-84		540	108
172	9788121256247	16th, Vol. XIV-A	Jullundur District, with maps and Kapurthala		1990	398
173	9788121256261	17th, Pt. I	Kangra (Proper)		1450	290
174	9788121256285	17th, Pt. II	Kangra (Kulu, Lahual, Spiti)		1800	357
175	9788121256308	18th	Karnal		1930	386
176	9788121256322	19th	Kohat		1540	307
177	9788121256346	20th	The Lahore District 1883-84		1220	244
178	9788121256384	21st	Ludhiana and Maler Kotla		1680	335
179	9788121256407	22nd	Lyallpur		735	147
180	9788121256421	23rd	Mianwali		1170	234
181	9788121256445	24th	Montgomery	P. J. Fagan	1590	318
182	9788121258364	25th	Multan (1901-02)	E. D. Maclagan	2400	480
183	9788121258708	26th	The Rohtak District 1883-84		980	196
184	9788121258746	27th, Vol. III A	Dujana State 1904		500	16
185	9788121256483	28th	Shahpur District		1780	356
186	9788121256506	29th	Simla District		800	159

S. NO.	ISBN NO.	VOLUME	TITLE	AUTHOR	PRICE	PAGES
187	9788121256520	30th	The Chamba State		2040	408
188	9788121256544	31st	The Chenab Colony 1904		1550	310
189	9788121256568	32nd	Kalsia State		270	53
190	9788121256582	33rd	Suket and Mandi		770	154
191	9788121256605	34th	Phulkian States, Patiala Jind And Nabha 1904		2070	414
192	9788121256643	35th	Simla Hill States		2220	443
193	9788121256667	36th	Sirmur		920	183
			RAJPUTANA DISTRICT GAZETTEERS			
194	9789362088994	1st, Vol. I-A & B	Ajmer-merwara (Text and Statistics Tables)	C. C. Watson	1230	246
195	9789362080882	2nd. Vol. II-A & B	Mewar Residency (Text and Statistics Tables)	K.D. Erskine	1700	339
196	9789362088444	3rd, Vol. III-A & B	The Western Rajputana States Residency And The Bikaner Agency	K.D. Erskine	3590	718
			UNITED PROVINCES OF AGRA AND OUDH DISTRICT GAZETTEERS			
197	9789362087560	Vol. I	Agra	H. R. Nevill	2260	452
198	9789362082466	Vol. II	Aligarh	H. R. Nevill	1300	260
199	9789362089779	Vol. III	Allahabad	H. R. Nevill	2050	409
200	9789362081346	Vol. IV	Almora	H. G. Walton	1670	333
201	9789362085658	Vol. V	Azamgarh	D. L. Drake Brockman	1750	349
202	9789362080547	Vol. VI	Bahraich	H. R. Nevill	1410	281
203	9789362085214	Vol. VII	Ballia	H. R. Nevill	1750	350
204	9789362084668	Vol. VIII	Banda	D. L. Drake Brockman	1750	349
205	9789362086518	Vol. IX	Bara Banki	H. R. Nevill	1720	344
206	9789362084101	Vol. X	Bareilly	H. R. Nevill	1640	327
207	9789362086631	Vol. XI	Basti	H. R. Nevill	1610	321
208	9789362083814	Vol. XII	Benares	H. R. Nevill	2290	458
209	9789362086105	Vol. XIII	Bijnor	H. R. Nevill	1820	363
210	9789362081674	Vol. XIV	Budaun	H. R. Nevill	1890	378
211	9789362086891	Vol. XV	Bulandshahr	H. R. Nevill	2100	419
212	9789362081520	Vol. XVI	Cawnpore	H. R. Nevill	2210	442
213	9789362088031	Vol. XVII	Dehra Dun	H. G. Walton	1710	342
214	9789362088710	Vol. XVIII	Etah	E. R. Neave	1600	320
215	9789362082992	Vol. XIX	Etawah	D. L. Drake Brockman	1390	277
216	9789362082220	Vol. XX	Farrukhabad	E. R. Neave	1620	324
217	9789362083869	Vol. XXI	Fatehpur	H. R. Nevill	1890	377
218	9789362085962	Vol. XXII	Fyzabad	H. R. Nevill	1700	339
219	9789362087997	Vol. XXIII	Garhwal	H. G. Walton	1270	254
220	9789362089892	Vol. XXIV	Ghazipur	H. R. Nevill	1600	320
221	9789362085436	Vol. XXV	Gonda	H. R. Nevill	1650	330
222	9789362080271	Vol. XXVI	Gorakhpur	H. R. Nevill	1890	378
223	9789362086129	Vol. XXVII	Hamirpur	D. L. Drake Brockman	1390	277
224	9789362087638	Vol. XXVIII	Hardoi	H. R. Nevill	1680	336
225	9789362081636	Vol. XXIX	Jalaun	D. L. Drake Brockman	1180	236
226	9789362084309	Vol. XXX	Jaunpur	H. R. Nevill	1750	350
227	9789362084187	Vol. XXXI	Jhansi	D. L. Drake Brockman	1960	391
228	9789362089168	Vol. XXXII	Kheri	H. R. Nevill	1650	330
229	9789362086778	Vol. XXXIII	Lucknow	H. R. Nevill	1760	352
230	9789362088635	Vol. XXXIV	Mainpuri	H. R. Nevill	1740	348
231	9789362080424	Vol. XXXV	Meerut	H. R. Nevill	2170	434
232	9789362081087	Vol. XXXVI	Mirzapur	D. L. Drake Brockman	2430	486
233	9789362085443	Vol. XXXVII	Moradabad	H. R. Nevill	1900	380
234	9789362082763	Vol. XXXVIII	Muttra	D. L. Drake Brockman	2140	428
235	9789362089915	Vol. XXXIX	Muzaffarnagar	H. R. Nevill	2260	451
236	9789362086143	Vol. XL	Naini Tal	H. R. Nevill	1890	377
237	9789362086761	Vol. XLI	Partabgarh	H. R. Nevill	1560	312
238	9789362081124	Vol. XLII	Pilibhit	H. R. Nevill	1570	314
239	9789362084453	Vol. XLIII	Rai Bareli	H. R. Nevill	1610	322
240	9789362088284	Vol. XLIV	Rampur	H. R. Nevill	1170	234
241	9789362083654	Vol. XLV	Saharanpur	H. R. Nevill	2190	438
242	9789362083142	Vol. XLVI	Shahjahanpur	H. R. Nevill	1510	302
243	9789362083623	Vol. XLVII	Sitapur	H. R. Nevill	1590	317
244	9789362089939	Vol. XLVIII	Sultanpur	H. R. Nevill	1330	266
245	9789362080851	Vol. XLIX	Unnao	H. R. Nevill	1530	305

MADRAS DISTRICT GAZETTEERS.

TINNEVELLY.

VOLUME II.

PRICE, 1 *rupee.*] [1 *shilling* 6 *pence.*

MADRAS DISTRICT GAZETTEERS.

STATISTICAL APPENDIX

FOR

TINNEVELLY DISTRICT.

MADRAS:
PRINTED BY THE SUPERINTENDENT, GOVERNMENT PRESS.

1915.

TABLE OF CONTENTS.

TABLE		PAGE
I.	Area, Population, etc., in 1911	1
II.	Variation in Population since 1891	2
III.	Roads	2
IV.	List of Travellers' Bungalows	3
V.	Religions in 1911	7
VI.	Vital Statistics	8
VII.	Causes of Death	10
VIII.	Castes, Tribes and Races in 1911	12
IX.	Classification of area and principal crops in Fasli 1322 (1912–13)	13
X.	Reserved Forest and area proposed for reservation on 30th June 1913	16
XI.	Classification of area and money rates according to the last settlement—	
	Part 1. Area under each money rate ..	17
	„ 2. Classes and sorts included under each money rate	20
XII.	Rainfall	22
XIII.	Holdings, Cultivation and Demand in Fasli 1322	24
XIV.	Revenue payable by permanently-settled estates in Fasli 1322 (1912-13)...	25
XV.	Demand, Collection and Balance of Current Land Revenue and Cesses	27
XVI.	Remissions	28
XVII.	Land Improvement and Agriculturists' Loans ...	29
XVIII.	Prices in seers per rupee	30
XIX.	Income-tax (Part IV. "Other sources only")...	35
XX.	Abkāri and Opium	37
XXI.	Revenue Receipts	38
XXII.	Sea-borne Trade—Total Trade in each port ...	39
XXII-A.	Sea-borne Trade—Chief Imports and Exports in selected ports	40
XXIII.	Income and Expenditure of Local Boards in 1912-13	44
XXIV.	Income and Expenditure of Municipalities in 1912-13	46
XXV.	Education in 1911	48
XXVI.	Schools and Scholars in 1912-13	49
XXVII.	Expenditure on Schools in 1912-13	50
XXVIII.	Hospitals and Dispensaries in 1912	51
XXIX.	Vaccination	53
XXX.	Civil Justice	53
XXXI.	Criminal Justice	54
XXXII.	Work of Criminal Courts	55
XXXIII.	Police and Jails in 1912	55

I.—Area, Population, etc., in 1911.

Locality.	Area in square miles.	Number of			Population, 1911.			Population (both sexes) in 1901.	Percentage of variation (of population).		Density of population per square mile, 1911.
		Towns.	Villages.	Occupied houses.	Total.	Males.	Females.		1891–1901.	1901–11.	
(1)	(2)	(3)	(4)	(5)	(6)	(7)	(8)	(9)	(10)	(11)	(12)
Sērmādēvi Division.											
Ambāsamudram	481	7	70	44,957	193,406	91,759	101,647	182,481	− 0·6	+ 6·0	402
Nānguněri	730	2	228	47,213	209,714	98,287	111,427	202,512	+ 16·1	+ 3·6	287
Tinnevelly Division.											
Tinnevelly	326	2	125	48,096	211,517	100,984	110,533	194,647	+ 5·4	+ 8·7	649
Tenkāsi	376	3	89	43,629	195,026	96,167	98,859	174,480	+ 12·6	+ 11·8	519
Tuticorin Division.											
Srīvaikuntam	361	3	94	48,848	201,899	96,872	105,027	165,600	+ 7·1	+ 21·9	559
Tiruchendūr	323	5	72	48,114	213,556	102,717	110,839	206,140	+ 14·7	+ 3·6	661
Kōilpatti Division.											
Kōilpatti	1,039	2	348	68,453	336,706	164,848	171,858	324,148	+ 4·6	+ 3·9	324
Sankaranainārkōil	717	4	114	49,255	228,795	113,999	114,796	208,542	+ 10·2	+ 9·7	319
District Total ...	4,353	28	1,140	398,065	1,790,619	865,633	924,986	1,658,405	+ 8·3	+ 8·0	411

II.—Variation in Population since 1891.

Towns.	Population.			Percentage of variation of population.	
	1911.	1901.	1891.	1891–1901.	1901–1911.
(1)	(2)	(3)	(4)	(5)	(6)
The whole District ...	1,790,619	1,658,495	1,531,049	+ 8·3	+ 8·0
Ambāsamudram Taluk—					
Kallidaikkurichi.	17,263	14,918	11,096	+ 34·4	+ 15·8
Vīravanallur ...	15,966	17,327	13,951	+ 24·2	− 7·9
Ambāsamudram.	14,207	12,869	9,944	+ 29·4	+ 10·4
Kadaiyam ...	13,798	12,917†	12,208†	+ 5·8	+ 6·8
Sermādevi ...	12,150	13,474	9,333	+ 44·4	− 9·8
Melacheval ...	10,071	10,379†	12,285†	− 15·5	− 8·0
Pattamadai ...	6,290	7,078†	8,086†	− 12·5	− 11·1
Nānguneri Taluk—					
Nānguneri	8,496	6,580	3,548	+ 85·5	+ 29·1
Vadakku Valliyūr.	7,661	6,903	4,907	+ 40·7	+ 11·0
Tinnevelly Taluk—					
Palamcottah * ...	44,909	39,545	18,686	+ 111·6	+ 13·6
Tinnevelly * ..	44,805	40,469	24,768	+ 63·4	+ 10·7
Tenkāsi Taluk—					
Tenkāsi	19,940	18,128	12,861	+ 40·9	+ 10·0
Kadaiyanallūr ...	17,077	13,939	8,200	+ 70·0	+ 22·5
Surandai	13,149	11,810	7,479	+ 57·9	+ 11·3
Srivaikuntam Taluk—					
Tuticorin * ...	40,185	28,048	25,107	+ 11·7	+ 43·3
Srivaikuntam ...	11,005	10,550	7,209	+ 46·3	+ 4·3
Siruthondanallūr ...	4,920	6,099	5,914	+ 3·1	− 19·3
Tiruchendūr Taluk—					
Tiruchendūr ...	25,531	26,056	8,266	+ 215·2	− 2·0
Kulasēkarapatnam.	21,812	19,898	15,924	+ 25·0	+ 9·6
Kāyalpatnam ...	12,862	11,746	11,465	+ 2·5	+ 9·5
Sāttānkulam ...	7,440	6,953	5,430	+ 28·0	+ 7·0
Azhvar Tirunagari...	6,820	6,630	5,077	+ 30·6	+ 2·9
Kōilpatti Taluk—					
Ettaiyāpuram ...	8,636	8,788	6,321	+ 39·0	− 1·7
Kōilpatti	5,016	3,415†	2,740†	+ 24·6	+ 46·9
Sankaranainārkōil Taluk—					
Puliyankudi ...	15,468	15,729†	13,818†	+ 13·8	− 1·7
Sankaranainār-kōil.	15,182	16,775	8,566	+ 95·8	− 9·5
Sivagiri	12,257	18,150	8,987	+ 102·0	− 32·5
Vāsudēvanallur.	9,882	8,878	7,790†	+ 14·0	+ 11·3

* Municipal town.
† Population entered represents that of the revenue villages which now make up the town. Such areas were not treated as urban in the censuses of those years.

III.—Roads.

Year.	Mileage of roads maintained.		
	Total.	Metalled.	Unmetalled.
(1)	(2)	(3)	(4)
1911–12	801	790	11

NOTE.—The omission of the previous years' figures from the table has been necessitat by the redistribution of administrative areas effected in the district in 1910.

IV.—List of Travellers' Bungalows.

Serial number.	Taluks and stations.	By whom maintained.	Nearest railway station, if any, and the distance from it.	Nature of accommodation.
(1)	(2)	(3)	(4)	(5)
	SĒRMĀDĒVI DIVISION.			
	Ambāsamudram Taluk.			
1	Kannadian Anicut * (Inspection bungalow).	P.W.D.	Ambāsamudram, 2 miles; Kallidaikkurichi, 1½ miles.	Tiled; one main room, bath room and dressing room; chairs and tables and one cot; kitchen and stables.
2	Mundanthurai * (in the forest, 550 ft.).	Forest Department.	Ambāsamudram, 9 miles.	Tiled; ground floor, one set of rooms; upstairs, one room and two bath rooms; chairs and tables; kitchen and stables.
3	Kannikatti * (on the hills, 2,500 ft.).	Do.	Ambāsamudram, 19½ miles.	Tiled; main room and two bath rooms; tables and chairs; kitchen and stables.
4	Sivasailam * ...	Do.	Azhvārkurichi, 4 miles	Tiled; two rooms, two bath rooms, kitchen and stables; furnished with chairs and tables.
5	Ambāsamudram † ...	Sērmādēvi Taluk Board.	Ambāsamudram, ½ mile.	Three rooms and bath rooms; furnished.
	Nanguneri Taluk.			
6	Tirukkurunkudi (Inspection shed).*	P.W.D.	Sērmādēvi, 19 miles.	Thatched; two rooms and bath room; tables, chairs and cot; stables and kitchen.
7	Kumāraswāmi Pillai‡ Anicut Bungalow (on Tirukkurunkudi hills).	Do.	Sērmādēvi, 30 miles.	Corrugated zinc roof; two rooms and two bath rooms; tables and chairs; kitchen and stables.
8	Kalakkād * (Inspection shed).	Do.	Sērmādēvi, 13 miles.	Thatched; main room, bath room and dressing room; tables, chairs and cot; kitchen and stables.

IV.—List of Travellers' Bungalows—*cont.*

Serial number. (1)	Taluks and stations. (2)	By whom maintained. (3)	Nearest railway station, if any, and the distance from it. (4)	Nature of accommodation. (5)
	SĒRMĀDĒVI DIVISION—*cont.*			
	Nanguneri Taluk—cont.			
9	Sivanāppēri (2 miles west of Kalakkād).*	Forest Department.	Sērmādēvi, 14 miles.	Tiled; two rooms and bath rooms; stables and kitchen; furnished with table and chairs.
10	Senkaltheri * (on the hills, 3,000 ft.).	Do.	Sērmadēvi, 24 miles.	Tiled; one main room, two side rooms and bath rooms and outhouse (kitchen and godowns); furnished with tables and chairs.
11	Nādukāni * (on the hills, 2,500 ft.).	Do.	Sērmādēvi, 26 miles.	Tiled; two rooms and two bath rooms and out-house (kitchen and godowns); furnished with tables and chairs.
12	Marukālkurichi † (Nāngunēri).	Sērmādēvi Taluk Board.	Tinnevelly Bridge, 18 miles.	Building with bomb proof roof; two rooms, two bath rooms and a kitchen and stable; furnished with chairs, tables and cots.
	TINNEVELLY DIVISION.			
	Tinnevelly Taluk.			
13	Kondūnakaram * (Inspection bungalow).	P.W.D.	Pēttai, 8 miles; Mēlakkathūr, 2 miles.	Tiled; one room with a bath and dressing room; furnished with chairs, tables and a cot; stable and kitchen.
14	Palamcottah ‡ ...	Palamcottah municipality.	Tinnevelly Bridge, 2 miles.	One large room and two small ones; fully furnished.
	Tenkāsi Taluk.			
15	Nannagaram * (Inspection shed).	P.W.D.	Tenkāsi, 2 miles.	Thatched; two rooms and a bath room; tables, chairs and a cot; stables and kitchen.

IV.—List of Travellers' Bungalows—*cont.*

Serial number. (1)	Taluks and stations (2)	By whom maintained. (3)	Nearest railway station, if any, and the distance from it. (4)	Nature of accommodation. (5)
	TINNEVELLY DIVISION—*cont.*			
	Tenkāsi Taluk—cont.			
16	Kuttālam ‡... ...	Forest Department	Tenkāsi, 4 miles.	Tiled building; one main room with two side rooms, two bath rooms, kitchen and godowns and stables and extra godowns; furnished with chairs and tables.
	TUTICORIN DIVISION.			
	Srīvaikuntam Taluk			
17	Kōrampallam (Inspection bungalow).*	P.W.D.	Tuticorin, 5 miles.	Tiled; one room, two bath rooms; chairs, tables and a cot; stable and kitchen.
18	Pudukkudi (Inspection bungalow).*	Do.	Tinnevelly bridge, 16 miles.	Tiled; two rooms and two bath rooms; tables, chairs and cots; stables and kitchen.
19	Vallanād (Inspection bungalow).	Do.	Tinnevelly bridge, 12 miles.	Tiled; one room, with verandah, one cook room thatched; no furniture; for subordinates only.
20	Do. *...	Forest Department.	Do.	Tiled; two rooms and bath room, stables and kitchen; furnished with chairs and tables.
21	Iruvappapuram (Inspection bungalow).*	P.W.D.	Tuticorin, 14 miles.	Tiled; one room, two bath rooms; cot, tables and chairs; kitchen and stables.
	Tiruchendūr Taluk.			
22	Poraiyūr (Inspection bungalow).*	Do.	Tinnevelly bridge, 25 miles.	Tiled; one room, two bath rooms; chairs and tables and cot; stables and kitchen.
23	Nāsareth *	Forest Department.	Tinnevelly bridge, 24 miles.	Tiled; two rooms, bath room; stables and kitchen; furnished with chairs and tables.

IV.—List of Travellers' Bungalows—*cont.*

Serial number. (1)	Taluks and stations. (2)	By whom maintained. (3)	Nearest railway station, if any, and the distance from it. (4)	Nature of accommodation. (5)
	KOILPATTI DIVISION.			
	Kōilpatti Taluk.			
24	Kāyattār †	Kōilpatti Taluk Board.	Kadambūr, 6 miles.	One terraced hall with two rooms; bath and kitchen rooms.
25	Kurukkuchalai § ...	Do.	Tuticorin, 10 miles.	One room and verandah.
26	Vēdanattam ‖ ...	Do.	Tuticorin, 15 miles.	Four very small rooms.
27	Kōilpatti †	Do.	Kōilpatti.	Two terraced halls with two rooms, one bath room and separate kitchen rooms.
	Sankaranainārkōil Taluk.			
28	Vāsudēvanallūr ‡ ...	Forest Department.	Tenkāsi, 22 miles.	Tiled; three rooms, two bath rooms, stable and kitchen; furnished with chairs and tables.
29	Sankaranainārkōil ‖.	Kōilpatti Taluk Board.	Kōilpatti, 24 miles; Tinnevelly bridge, 34 miles.	Tiled; two rooms, two bath rooms, one kitchen and a stable.

Charges per diem.

* As. 8 for a single person; for married couple As. 12.
† One rupee for the first day; As. 8 for subsequent days for each adult; for married couple one and a half times the single rate.
‡ Rupee one for a single person; Rs. 1-8-0 for married couple.
§ Free.
‖ As. 8 for the first day and As. 4 for subsequent days for each adult. } For married couple times the single rate.

V.—Religions in 1911.

Taluks.	Hindus.			Mussalmans.			Christians.			Others.		
	Total.	Males.	Females.	Total.	Males.	Females.	Total.	Males.	Females.	Total.	Males.	Females.
(1)	(2)	(3)	(4)	(5)	(6)	(7)	(8)	(9)	(10)	(11)	(12)	(13)
Sērmādēvi Division.												
Ambāsamudram	172,389	81,862	90,527	10,753	4,915	5,838	10,264	4,982	5,282	...	...	...
Nāngunēri	162,487	76,258	86,229	10,667	4,910	5,757	36,560	17,119	19,441	...	...	...
Tinnevelly Division.												
Tinnevelly	174,189	83,459	90,730	24,277	11,092	13,185	13,034	6,418	6,616	17	15	2
Tenkāsi	168,054	82,917	85,137	18,151	8,811	9,340	8,820	4,438	4,382	1	1	...
Tuticorin Division.												
Srivaikuntam	166,554	80,251	86,303	10,676	4,599	6,077	24,655	12,011	12,644	14	11	3
Tiruchendūr	143,585	72,314	71,271	20,614	7,467	13,147	49,357	22,936	26,421	...	...	...
Kōilpatti Division.												
Kōilpatti	309,384	151,539	157,845	5,727	2,767	2,960	21,595	10,542	11,053	...	...	...
Sankaranainārkōil	213,582	106,847	106,735	4,609	2,292	2,317	11,604	5,860	5,744	...	...	...
District Total ...	1,509,224	734,447	774,777	105,474	46,853	58,621	175,889	84,306	91,583	32	27	5

VI.—Vital Statistics.

Taluks.	Ratio per 1,000 of population of																			
	Births.										Deaths.									
	1903.	1904.	1905.	1906.	1907.	1908.	1909.	1910.	1911.	1912.	1903.	1904.	1905.	1906.	1907.	1908.	1909.	1910.	1911.	1912.
(1)	(2)	(3)	(4)	(5)	(6)	(7)	(8)	(9)	(10)	(11)	(12)	(13)	(14)	(15)	(16)	(17)	(18)	(19)	(20)	(21)
SĒRMĀDĒVI DIVISION.																				
Ambāsamudram	...	...	...	...	...	...	...	50·6	48·6	48·9	...	...	...	...	...	...	...	40·1	42·2	43·0
Nānguneri	...	...	...	...	...	...	...	30·1	32·4	31·2	...	...	...	...		...	...	21·4	23·4	26·4
TINNEVELLY DIVISION.																				
Tinnevelly	...	...	...	...	...	...	...	33·9	38·6	33·9	...	...	...	...	...	...	...	24·0	29·1	27·1
Tenkāsi	...	...	...		...	...	...	41·9	38·2	38·2	...	...		...	...	...	...	28·6	30·4	29·8
TUTICORIN DIVISION.																				
Srīvaikuntam	...	...	...	...	...	...		36·7	30·6	27·2	...	...	...	...	...	...	...	23·3	27·6	25·3
Tiruchendūr	...	...	...	...	...	...	...	34·5	39·0	37·6	...	...	...	...	...	...	...	32·8	39·5	37·8
KOILPATTI DIVISION.																				
Kōilpatti	...	...	...	...	...			31·1	25·5	24·9	...	...	...	...	...	...	...	20·9	24·1	18·1
Sankaranainārkōil	...	...	...	...	...	...	...	32·8	32·9	32·9	...	...	...	...	...	...	...	17·6	20·5	20·5
TOWN CIRCLES.																				
Palamcottah Municipality	41·3	44·3	45·1	48·9	42·5	41·2	42·5	42·5	36·4	37·5	30·2	28·3	30·0	40·9	30·3	34·7	31·2	34·1	30·6	28·7
Tinnevelly do.	35·6	40·4	39·9	37·2	38·2	37·8	39·6	38·0	35·1	36·2	28·5	31·1	31·5	42·6	34·1	43·1	31·4	35·3	34·0	32·0
Tuticorin do. ...	29·6	33·6	33·6	36·8	36·9	35·8	38·7	28·3	28·3	34·5	34·6	28·4	30·1	43·0	51·3	34·8	31·3	35·4	34·4	36·6
Tiruchendūr	11·7	11·3	10·4	9·9	9·6	14·2	11·6	10·6	9·8	13·0	11·0	9·1	9·5	8·7	7·9	11·8	9·9	16·7	18·2	12·1
Kulasēkarapatnam	28·5	34·0	28·2	24·2	20·1	26·6	28·7	25·8	24·9	22·6	19·8	20·0	18·7	15·1	18·0	21·1	18·2	21·5	27·4	31·6

Tenkāsi	40·3	41·5	35·9	37·9	39·7	35·5	38·7	42·7	32·0	37·4	30·1	24·5	24·4	39·4	31·1	35·1	27·3	36·0	23·2	26·8
Kallidaikkurichi	40·8	41·6	34·3	32·9	33·3	35·5	35·5	39·4	28·2	30·0	27·5	28·8	29·0	37·1	25·8	30·0	27·1	30·8	25·7	24·4
Kadaivanallūr	48·4	42·5	42·5	39·6	37·0	41·9	34·8	38·2	30·2	29·9	25·0	22·3	28·0	26·0	24·8	32·9	16·9	24·4	16·9	17·6
Vīravanallūr	39·0	37·5	32·1	34·8	30·1	17·9	28·5	33·2	36·6	29·6	30·6	28·8	24·6	37·7	24·9	19·4	20·7	31·8	35·5	25·4
Puliyankudi *	...	...	...	...	...	..	..	...	25·3	20·5	...	...	...	...	...		...	...	12·7	12·7
Sankaranainārkōil	33·2	39·9	34·2	32·5	27·2	27·2	21.1	32·0	39·4	38·2	21·0	22·8	22·8	25·2	16·0	13·8	10·4	20·4	24·5	23·1
Ambāsamudram	29·1	34·3	31·5	23·2	21·1	25·5	25·7	22·3	24·8	21·8	29·2	26·8	24·9	25·6	19·5	29·5	23·2	26·4	28·4	26·0
Kadaiyam *	...	...	...		..	...	...	...	24·0	20·2	..	...	...	...		...	...	...	28·3	10·7
Surandai	29·9	41·7	30·8	35·0	38·5	37·9	30·7	32·4	30·9	30·9	22·4	21·6	23·5	35·9	24·0	23·8	17·6	22·4	24·5	18·0
Kāyalpatnam	14.0	17·4	15·8	17·4	28·4	19·7	21·3	21·5	21·5	21·1	19·9	13·7	14·2	16·2	24·2	19·8	21·1	28·7	41·8	39·9
Sivagiri	17·7	20·8	23·8	10·3	18·7	22·4	17·9	24·2	31·7	28·7	12·6	11·3	12·7	16·6	12·5	9·9	8·4	11·1	20·3	21·5
Sērmādēvi	37·6	35·1	23·5	32·4	29·5	29·9	25·5	30·3	34·5	34·5	25·5	25·8	24·9	28·7	29·2	26·4	23·2	28·8	29·9	30·0
Srīvaikuntam	34·2	34·9	41·8	32·6	41·9	40·7	43·6	41·1	38·1	35·4	30·1	28·4	22·7	41·0	43·4	47·5	28·0	35·5	28·5	30·5
Mēlacheval *	...	...	...	...	..	...	...	...	34·7	25·2	...	...	..	...	..	...	...	...	34·7	19·7
Vāsudēvanallūr *	...	...	..	...	...	...	...	...	31·4	8·4	..	...	..	...	...	...	...	...	19·5	8·6
Ettaiyāpuram	...	21·4	21·1	14·0	7·3	38·5	24·6	22·6	16·1	13·3	...	14·0	18·4	13·2	5·8	34·5	21·5	17·9	10·8	8·8
Nāngunēri	...	42·1	36·5	46·2	46·4	27·5	24·9	33·0	25·7	28·6	...	34·8	29·3	37·5	37·7	24·6	20·1	29·9	25·7	20·7
Vadakku Valliyūr	...	38·1	39·1	38·1	36·8	44·6	27·2	34·0	28·7	[illegible]	...	24·6	17·8	44·9	18·8	24·3	23·2	22·8	17·0	26·5
Sattānkulam	...	32·1	35·7	37·3	23·1	28·0	28·9	31·5	25·4	19·4	...	18·1	22·3	26·6	14·1	16·8	17·4	18·0	30·1	38·7
Azhvār Tirunagari	...	34·4	37·1	33·2	30·8	32·7	32·6	28·1	33·6	33·1	...	25·9	30·2	37·9	36·0	51·4	25·6	39·2	36·1	28·7
Pattamadai *	...	...	...	...	...	...	...	...	36·9	17·3	...	...	...	...	...	...	...	...	35·1	16·7
Kōilpatti *	...	...	...	...	...	...	...	...	21·5	22·1	...	.	...	...	...	...	...	...	16·5	16·3
Siruthondanallūr	...	36·6	38·2	44·1	44·4	44·9	47·4	43·8	...	..	..	27·5	20·3	54·9	33·9	53·3	24·9	26·7	...	.
Total for the District ..	...	...	...	...	...	...	..	34·6	32·8	31·6	...	...	...	...	...	...	...	25·5	27·8	26·2

* Treated as Town from 1911 only.

NOTE.—(a) This table excludes the statistics relating to Europeans and Eurasians.

(b) For taluks and whole district, the omission of the figures prior to 1910 has been necessitated by the redistribution of administrative areas effected in 1910.

VII.—Causes of Death.

(Average of the statistics for the three years ending 1912.)

Taluks.	Ratio of deaths per 1,000 of population from						Total.
	Cholera.	Small-pox.	Plague.	Fever.	Dysentery and Diarrhœa.	All other causes.	
(1)	(2)	(3)	(4)	(5)	(6)	(7)	(8)
Sērmādēvi Division.							
Ambāsamudram	3·2	0·1	...	6·6	1·1	30·8	41·8
Nāngunēri	1·7	0·1	...	5·4	0·5	16·1	23·8
Tinnevelly Division.							
Tinnevelly	2·0	0·2	...	3·8	0·9	20·5	27·4
Tenkāsi	2·7	0·2	..	5·4	0·9	20·4	29·6
Tuticorin Division.							
Srīvaikuntam	2·7	0·2	...	7·4	1·1	14·0	25·4
Tiruchendūr	4·4	0·1	...	10·8	1·0	20·4	36·7
Kōilpatti Division.							
Kōilpatti	1·2	0·3	...	4·1	0·7	14·7	21·0
Sankaranainārkōil ...	2·0	0·1	...	3·3	0·7	13·4	19·5
Town Circles.							
Palamcottah Municipality ...	2·8	0·2	...	1·9	13·3	12·9	31·1
Tinnevelly do. ...	2·9	1·0	..	2·4	3·5	24·0	33·8
Tuticorin do. ...	4·8	1·5	...	4·5	7·2	17·5	35·5
Tiruchendūr	3·2	...	...	3·1	0·6	8·1	14·0
Kulasēkarapatnam ...	1·5	...	...	10·7	0·2	14·4	26·8
Tenkāsi	2·5	...	...	4·3	2·6	19·3	28·7
Kallidaikkurichi	...	...	...	5·8	3·3	17·8	26·9
Kadaiyanallūr	2·4	...	...	5·2	1·7	10·3	19·6
Vīravanallūr	1·1	...	...	4·6	0·2	25·0	30·9
Puliyankudi *	0·1	...		4·6	0·3	7·7	12·7
Sankaranainārkōil ..	1·1	...	...	5·9	1·4	14·3	22·7
Ambāsamudram	2·8	...	...	3·0	2·4	18·7	26·9
Kādaiyam *	2·5	0·05	...	1·4	0·1	12·9	17·0
Surandai ..	1·8	...	...	6·7	1·7	11·4	21·6
Kāyalpatnam	4·9	0·07	...	13·5	1·9	16·4	36·8
Sivagiri	2·9	...	...	0·1	...	14·6	17·6
Sērmādēvi	1·1	0·07	...	5·1	3·9	19·4	29·6
Srīvaikuntam	3·3	...	...	1·2	...	27·0	31·5
Mēla cheval * ...	1·1	0·1	...	4·2	0·9	20·9	27·2

* Average of the two years 1911 and 1912.

VII.—Causes of Death—*cont.*

(Average of the statistics for the three years ending 1912.)

Taluks.	Ratio of deaths per 1,000 of population from						Total.
	Cholera.	Small-pox.	Plague.	Fever.	Dysentery and Diarrhœa.	All other causes.	
(1)	(2)	(3)	(4)	(5)	(6)	(7)	(8)
TOWN CIRCLES—*cont.*							
Vāsudēvanallūr *	0·3	0·1	..	3·9	0·2	9·5	14·0
Ettaiyāpuram	0·3	...	...	2·4	0·4	9·4	12·5
Nāngunēri	1·5	0·07		7·6	1·1	18·1	28·4
Vadakkuvalliyūr	1·7	...	...	3·9	0.1	16·2	21·9
Sāttānkulam	10·7	0·2	...	3·8	0·3	13·9	28·9
Azhvar Tirunagari... ...	1·8	0·2	...	5·9	0·7	26·0	34·6
Pattamadai *	1·5	...	...	2·0	1·2	21·2	25·9
Kōilpatti *	1·2	...	..	0·5	0·1	14·6	16·4
Total for the District ...	2·3	0·2	...	5·3	1·4	17·3	26·5

* Average of the two years 1911 and 1912.

NOTE.—(1) This table excludes the statistics relating to Europeans and Eurasians.

(2) The average figures of the three years ending 1912 are given in this table since the figures prior to 1910 relate to the old Tinnevelly district.

VIII.—Castes, Tribes and Races in 1911.

Caste, Tribe or Race.	Strength.
I.—Hindu and Animist Castes	
(a) *Tamil.*	
Shānān	271,[illegible]09
Pallan	193,219
Maravan	176,713
Vellālan	168,076
Paraiyan	98,431
Idaiyan	96,554
Kammālan	79,204
Brāhman	49,337
Vāniyan	24,979
Vannān	24,951
Kaikōlan	21,899
Ambattan	20,308
Chetti	9,574
Kusavan	8,823
Pandāram	8,629
Kuravan	5,032
Īluvan	4,510
Valaiyan	2,682
Total (a) ..	1,264,180
(b) *Telugu.*	
Kamma	52,938
Balija	32,929
Chakkiliyan	29,155
Kāpu	21,279
Tottiyan	9,939
Sālo	5,156
Brāhman	4,632
Rāzu	1,861
Total (b) ...	157,939
(c) *Other Madras Languages.*	
Patnulkaran	4,249
Kshatriya	2,429
Total (c) ...	6,678

Caste, Tribe or Race.	Strength.
(d) Other Castes not specified under Tamil, Telugu, Malayalam, Canarese, Oriya and other Madras languages.	80,477
Total (d) ...	80,477
Total I. ...	1,509,224
II.—Mussalman Tribes.	
Labbai	
Sheik	49,451
Saiyad	32,107
Pathan	5,456
Others	2,149
	16,311
Total II. .	105,474
III.—Christian Races.	
Indian Christian	175,492
Anglo Indian	153
English	213
Others	31
Total III. ...	175,889
IV.—Others ...	32
District Total ...	1,790,619

Note.—Castes, Tribes or Races contributing less than one per mille to the district population are not shown separately in this table but included under the term "Others."

IX.—Classification of area and principal crops in fasli 1322 (1912–13)

Items.	Sērmādēvi Division.		Tinnevelly Division.		Tuticorin Division.		Kōilpatti Division.		District Total.
	Ambā-samudram.	Nāngu-nēri.	Tinnevelly.	Tenkāsi.	Srīvaikun-tam.	Tiruchen-dūr.	Kōilpatti.	Sankarn-nainār-kōil.	
(1)	(2)	(3)	(4)	(5)	(6)	(7)	(8)	(9)	(10)
	ACS.	ACS.	ACS.	ACS.	ACS.	ACS.	ACS.	ACS.	ACS.
Government (Ryotwari) Land ... }	309,171	422,496	188,495	144,827	281,123	197,388	205,543	182,099	1,875,642
Minor inam ... ... }									
Whole inam	2,547	21,491	24,826	...	18,707	9,314	29,184	50,266	156,365
Zamindari	6,701	...	...	114,681	28,582	...	430,528	156,205	736,697
Total area by Survey ...	318,419	443,987	208,321	259,008	278,412	206,782	665,255	388,570	2,768,704
Forests	89,389	55,869	4,837	25,571	5,920	15,811	2,996	27,289	227,682
Not available for cultivation ...	38,130	18,561	39,039	37,570	37,534	28,675	167,017	109,869	476,395
Culturable waste other than fallow.	876	8,815	3,511	2,877	...	4,673	9,567	17,197	47,516
Current fallows	55,698	165,607	70,046	51,728	64,176	53,961	30,718	54,526	546,455
Net area cropped	76,186	143,887	87,172	143,890	120,276	100,159	500,448	225,036	1,397,049
Area shown in village accounts ...	260,279	392,739	204,605	261,636	227,906	203,279	710,736	433,917	2,695,097
Irrigated by Government canals ...	19,811	8,078	8,377	4,711	6,726	1,993	135	917	45,748
Do. by private canals... ...	...	...	...	...	...	...	...	...	...
Do. by tanks	17,371	33,848	22,958	32,649	21,233	17,988	8,746	32,076	186,869
Do. by wells	1,449	3,064	3,984	45,541	1,131	2,432	18,478	33,358	109,987
Do. by other sources	323	281	...	..	104	2,427	52	1	3,188
Total area irrigated ...	38,954	45,271	35,319	82,601	29,194	24,840	22,411	66,352	345,742

IX.—Classification of area and principal crops in fasli 1322 (1912–13)—*cont.*

Items.	Sērmādevi Division.		Tinnevelly Division.		Tuticorin Division.		Kōilpatti Division.		District Total.
	Ambā-samudram.	Nāngu-nēri.	Tinnevelly.	Tenkāsi.	Srivaikun-tam.	Tiruchen-dūr.	Kōilpatti.	Sankara-nainār-kōvil.	
(1)	(2)	(3)	(4)	(5)	(6)	(7)	(8)	(9)	(10)
Area under—									
Cereals and pulses—	ACS.	ACS.	ACS.	ACS.	ACS.	ACS.	ACS.	ACS.	ACS.
Rice	64,341	48,744	51,484	41,187	46,524	80,171	10,457	35,500	328,308
Cholam	1,165	9,921	3,770	36,001	1,454	595	40,075	24,180	117,161
Cambu	143	4,907	6,568	1,382	28,057	4,744	173,000	28,476	242,227
Ragi	858	1,662	2,083	6,388	1,098	904	10,809	14,233	37,985
Others	24,048	71,866	22,442	78,048	15,411	28,366	51,923	82,408	869,507
Total ...	90,555	187,100	86,297	162,856	92,544	59,780	286,264	179,792	1,095,188
Oil-Seeds—									
Til or gingelly	13,727	8,007	9,284	16,507	2,263	6,094	2,448	11,818	70,138
Ground nut	...	4	8	6	...	21	158	47	239
Castors	70	205	315	281	426	882	379	559	2 617
Others	17	11	8	169	1	1	...	11	218
Total ...	13,814	8,227	9,610	16,963	2,690	6,498	2,980	12,480	78,212
Condiments and spices	432	800	894	3,920	934	459	14,520	2,760	24,719
Sugarcane, etc.	1,477	3,123	2,890	466	8,375	26,305	536	494	43,666
Cotton	515	9,798	9,422	7,530	29,821	2,254	178,163	47,434	284,937
Indigo	534	112	102	127	20	100	16	14	1,025

Drugs and Narcotics—									
Tobacco	7	267	...	18	12	1	495	123	923
Others	810	268	8,722	726	1,562	469	26	277	12,360
Total ...	817	535	8,722	744	1,574	470	521	400	13,283
Fodder crops	18	154	1,663	932	6,219	32	22,026	10,463	41,503
Orchards and garden produce ...	1,819	2,172	1,161	8,293	1,821	8,212	1,771	2,414	17,663
Miscellaneous non-food crops ...	981	6,066	245	197	3,817	20,921	1,774	16	34,017
Total area cropped ...	110,457	168,087	121,006	197,028	147,815	120,031	508,571	256,217	1,629,212
Deduct area cropped more than once.	34,271	24,200	33,834	53,138	27,539	19,872	8,128	31,181	232,163
Net area cropped ...	76,186	143,887	87,172	143,890	120,276	100,159	500,443	225,036	1,397,049

X.—Reserved Forest and Area proposed for reservation (in square miles) on the 30th June 1913.

Taluks. (1)	Reserved Forest. (2)	Area proposed for reservation. (3)	Total of Columns 2 and 3. (4)	Area of taluk. (5)	Percentage of Column 4 to cultivated area. (6)
Sērmādēvi Division.					
Ambāsamudram	139·670	0·003	139·673	497·53	117·3
Nāngunēri	87·290	0·002	87·292	693·73	38·8
Tinnevelly Division.					
Tinnevelly	7·560	...	7·560	325·50	5·5
Tenkāsi	39·840	0·113	39·953	404·70	17·7
Tuticorin Division.					
Srīvaikuntam	9·250	...	9·250	435·02	4·9
Tiruchendūr	24·670	0·032	24·702	323·02	15·7
Kōilpatti Division.					
Kōilpatti	4·680	...	4·680	1,039·46	0·5
Sankaranainārkōil	42·640	...	42·640	607·14	12·1
District Total ...	355·600	0·150	355·750	4,326·10	16·3

Net revenue realised under Forests during 1911–12 is Rs. 33,454.
Do. do. 1912–13 is Rs. 51,557.

NOTE.—The omission of the previous years' figures under "Net Revenue" has been necessitated by the redistribution of the administrative areas of the district effected in 1910.

XI.—Classification of area and money rates according to the re-settlement.

(Part 1. Area under each money rate.)

Dry.

Particulars of money rates.	Sērmādēvi Division.		Tinnevelly Division.		Tuticorin Division.		Kōilpatti Division.		District Total.
	Ambāsamudram Taluk.	Nānguneri Taluk.	Tinnevelly Taluk.	Tenkāsi Taluk.	Srivaikuntam Taluk.	Tiruchendūr Taluk.	Kōilpatti Taluk.	Sankaranāyinārkōil Taluk.	
(1)	(2)	(3)	(4)	(5)	(6)	(7)	(8)	(9)	(10)
RS. A.	ACS.	ACS.	ACS.	ACS.	ACS.	ACS.	ACS.	ACS.	ACS.
2 13	26	6	6	..	144	177	...	1,101	1,460
1 11	252	684	289	1,783	14,620	847	32,842	22,107	73,324
1 2	747	929	3,730	8,692	13,638	3,285	45,696	20,075	96,792
0 13	2,100	675	2,036	26,618	5,999	3,226	32,287	19,677	92,650
0 9	10,691	5,760	13,483	9,194	15,946	3,969	21,176	20,330	100,549
0 6	14,973	37,826	21,702	10,308	23,033	14,023	20,210	39,287	181,362
0 4	55,768	179,753	66,064	7,174	36,408	55,019	12,285	1,559	407,430
0 3	..	23,467	...	...		37,038	1,566	...	62,071
Total ..	84,557	242,100	107,312	63,799	110,088	117,584	166,062	124,136	1,015,638
Special rates ...	...	39	...	82	468	...	..	34	623
Grand Total .	84,557	242,139	107,312	63,881	110,556	117,584	166,062	124,170	1,016,261

XI.—Classification of area and money rates according to the re-settlement—*cont.*

(Part 1. Area under each money rate.)

Wet.

Particulars of money rates.	Sērmādēvi Division.		Tinnevelly Division.		Tuticorin Division.		Kōilpatti Division.		District Total.
	Ambāsamudram.	Nānguneri.	Tinnevelly.	Tenkāsi.	Srīvaikuntam.	Tiruchendūr.	Kōilpatti.	Sankaranāyinārkōil.	
(1)	(2)	(3)	(4)	(5)	(6)	(7)	(8)	(9)	(10)
(a) *Single crop.*	ACS.	ACS.	ACS.	ACS.	ACS.	ACS.	ACS.	ACS.	ACS.
RS. A.									
15 0	...	...	...	...	...	..	...	..	...
13 2	5	..	2	...	...	...	...	...	7
11 8	..	...	...	...	...	1	...		1
10 4	...	2,195	...	...	...	...	...	...	2,195
10 2	48	...	2	..	131	...	...	...	181
8 8	126	...	90	141	24	650	...	1,208	2,234
7 8	100	6,683	13	..	86	...	...	...	6,837
6 12	393	11,979	1,480	825	624	1,921	334	3,514	20,520
5 10	45	...	86	...	8	...	...	...	134
5 0	847	3,416	2,450	517	2,380	2,218	1,268	5,132	18,178
4 0	1,085	807	783	255	684	712	776	1,958	6,510
3 6	367	34	68	7	356	46	194	190	1,262
2 12	27	18	...	2	67	45	24	12	195
2 4	4	10	...	...	.	..	21	...	35
Total ...	2,997	24,597	4,924	1,247	4,805	5,588	2,617	12,009	58,284

(b) *Double crop.*

22 8	4,372	...	3,247	...	..	...	...		7,619
19 12	3,672	...	3,562	240	5,750	...	...	..	13,224
17 8	602	...	...	..	192	2,045	...	...	2,839
15 4	5,404	1,982	4,068	687	5,595	1,687	...	...	19,373
14 6	166	949	...	...	4	1,615	...	...	2,734
11 6	1,164	494	991	1,451	1,123	1,968	...	51	7,242
11 4	2,461	...	2,304	401	3,854	...	...	...	9,020
10 10	516	1,235	170	617	41	2,821	...	...	5,400
10 4	87	...	..	...	...	...	...	...	87
9 0	1,164	483	1,022	2,957	1,772	729	...	108	8,235
8 8	3,438	928	2,881	1,546	668	2,098	...	198	11,752
8 2	26	460	86	...	378	686	...	5	1,686
6 10	266	...	298	3,190	816	246	...	40	4,856
6 6	1,453	...	78	108	227	...	...	...	1,866
6 4	484	59	2,098	2,686	193	860	...	561	7,841
6 0	348	81	415	125	369	1,602	9	20	2,969
5 4	454	...	280	3,160	...	...	...	114	4,008
5 0	589	16	1,582	808	52	...	...	118	3,115
4 12	1,643	264	384	452	98	508	27	111	8,487
4 8	64	...	..	46	...	...	..	3	113
4 4	125	...	60	108	...	...	...	7	300
4 0	593	13	140	83	24	...	121		913
3 8	...	...	16	...	...	...	..	...	16
3 4	82	...	5	18	...	...	12	...	117
2 10	...	87	2	...	...	.	...	..	89
Total ...	29,018	7,050	24,539	18,683	21,151	16,815	169	1,881	118,751
Special rates ...	503	1,147	173	309	206	105	466	821	8,730
Grand Total ...	32,518	32,794	29,636	20,239	25,662	22,508	8,252	14,161	180,765

XI.—Classification of area and money rates according to the re-settlement—*cont.*

(Part 2. Classes and sorts included under each money rate.)

Dry.				Wet.													
Soil.				Soil.		Classes of irrigation sources.											
						First Class.			Second Class.			Third Class.			Fourth Class.		
Class.	Sort.	Taram.	Rate.	Class.	Sort.	Taram.	Single crop. Rate.	Double crop. Rate.	Taram.	Single crop. Rate.	Double crop. Rate.	Taram.	Single crop. Rate.	Double crop. Rate.	Taram.	Single crop. Rate.	Double crop. Rate.
(1)	(2)	(3)	(4)	(5)	(6)	(7)	(8)	(9)	(10)	(11)	(12)	(13)	(14)	(15)	(16)	(17)	(18)
			RS. A.				RS. A.	RS. A.		RS. A.	RS. A.		RS. A.	RS. A.		RS. A.	RS. A.
IV	1	1	2 13														
• VII	A			IV	1	1	15 0	22 8	2	13 2	17 8	8	11 8	14 6	5	8 8	10 4
III	1			VII	A								†10 4				
IV	2	2	1 11	IV	2	2	13 2	19 12	3	11 8	15 4	5	8 8	10 10	7	6 12	8 2
VII	1			VII	1					‡10 4							
III	2			III	1												
IV	3			IV	3												
V	1	3	1 2	V	1	4	10 2	15 4	5	8 8	11 6	7	6 12	8 8	9	5 0	6 0
VII	2			VII	2												
VIII	1			VIII	1												
III	3			III	2												
IV	4			IV	4												
V	2	4	0 13	V	2	6	7 8	11 4	7	6 12	9 0	9	5 0	6 4	11	4 0	4 12
VII	3			VII	3												
VIII	2			VIII	2												

III	4			III	3												
IV	5			IV	5												
V	* 3	5	0 9	V	8	8	5 10	8 8	9	5 0	6 10	11	4 0	5 0	12	8 6	4 0
VII	4			VII	4												
VIII	8			VIII	3												
III	5			III	4												
V	4	6	0 6	V	4	10	4 4	6 6	11	4 0	5 4	12	3 6	4 4	13	2 12	3 4
VII	5			VII	5												
VIII	4			VIII	4												
V	5			III	5												
VIII	5	7	0 4	V	5	12	3 6	5 0	12	3 6	4 8	18	2 12	3 8	14	2 4	2 10
VIII	6	8	0 3	VIII	5												

* The VII-A dry classification applies to Koilpatti and Sankarannainarkoil taluks only.

† This classification and rate is in force only in the taluks of Nanguneri, Koilpatti and Sankarannainarkoil.

‡ Relates to Nanguneri taluk.

N.B.—(1) *First class* sources as a rule comprise riverfed sources, 85 per cent. of the area under which is regularly cultivated with two wet crops.

(2) *Second class* sources comprise riverfed sources, 50 to 85 per cent. of the area under which is regularly cultivated with two irrigated crops one of which is a wet crop.

(3) *Third class* sources comprise all riverfed sources, less than 50 per cent. of the area under which is cultivated with two irrigated crops and all rainfed sources affording five months' supply or more.

(4) *Fourth class* sources usually comprise rainfed sources affording less than five months' supply.

XII.—Rainfall.

Names of rain-gauge stations.	Average rainfall (1883-1912) in inches in												
	January.	February.	March.	April.	May.	June.	July.	August.	September.	October.	November.	December.	Whole year.
(1)	(2)	(3)	(4)	(5)	(6)	(7)	(8)	(9)	(10)	(11)	(12)	(13)	(14)
AMBASAMUDRAM TALUK.													
Kadaiyam (a)	1·34	1·68	1·64	1·75	0·96	1·86	1·90	0·57	0·60	8·13	6·98	3·68	31·29
Ambasamudram	1·87	1·73	2·04	2·10	1·72	1·28	0·67	0·51	0·41	6·95	9·09	6·16	34·53
NANGUNERI TALUK.													
Nanguneri	1·41	0·98	1·49	1·96	1·59	1·20	0·48	0·67	0·85	7·12	7·49	4·41	29·89
Radhapuram	0·71	0·79	1·36	1·88	1·06	2·05	1·17	0·44	0·47	6·60	6·85	3·58	30·06
Kuthankuli (b)	0·88	1·11	0·80	1·87	0·60	2·24	1·04	0·41	0·35	5·24	6·66	3·67	24·92
Sattankulam (c)	0·35	0·72	0·49	1·03	0·99	0·43	0·21	0·65	0·42	7·89	6·47	3·31	22·85
TINNEVELLY TALUK.													
Palamcottah	0·80	0·01	1·15	2·49	1·68	0·63	0·35	0·52	1·08	7·38	6·92	3·73	27·63
Tinnevelly (d)	0·65	...	0·71	5·15	3·99	0·84	0·00	0·20	0·96	11·39	3·81	2·25	29·95
TENKASI TALUK.													
Kadaiyanallur (e)	1·06	1·07	2·22	1·71	[illegible]	2·15	1·58	0·95	0·35	7·83	6·00	3·84	30·02
Tenkasi	1·89	1·63	2·48	3·25	1·67	4·27	3·32	1·42	0·80	7·63	7·87	4·56	40·75
SRIVAIKUNTAM TALUK.													
Arasadi (b)	1·02	0·74	1·12	1·76	0·88	0·25	0·19	0·25	0·57	6·89	6·10	2·78	2·55
Tuticorin	0·76	0·69	0·89	1·83	1·05	0·24	0·13	0·25	0·61	6·50	7·18	3·11	23·24
Kiranur (f)	1·56	0·46	0·72	1·45	0·55	0·17	0·14	0·09	0·22	5·50	6·56	2·92	20·34
Srivaikuntam	0·79	0·61	1·13	1·59	1·45	0·33	0·24	0·01	0·92	7·44	6·70	3·35	25·15
TIRUCHENDUR TALUK.													
Kulasekarapatnam	1·01	0·97	1·16	1·58	0·50	0·24	0·17	0·12	0·20	5·00	8·07	5·23	25·74

Koilpatti Taluk.													
Vilattikulam	0·50	0·71	0·93	1·63	1·21	0·31	0·31	1·59	2·00	7·78	5·38	2·50	24·80
Ottappidaram	0·01	0·62	0·64	1·79	1·44	0·57	0·29	0·88	1·63	7·99	6·37	2·82	25·05
Kayattur (g)	0·72	0·48	0·68	2·70	1·66	0·32	0·50	1·83	0·87	7·81	6·03	1·57	25·17
Koilpatti (h)	0·59	0·52	0·32	2·80	2·32	0·80	0·90	1·38	2·42	8·36	0·16	1·93	28·59
Sankaranainarkoil Taluk.													
ankaranainarkoil	0·66	0·95	1·56	2·91	1·83	0·63	0·32	0·52	0·89	7·29	3·60	2·89	26·05
Sivagiri (e)	1·17	2·10	2·43	2·56	1·64	0·87	1·15	1·24	1·09	9·90	7·84	3·41	35·40
District Total	0·93	0·96	1·35	2·09	1·31	1·00	0·63	0·64	0·85	7·09	7·09	3·79	27·7

(a) 1907—1912. (b) 1894—1912. (c) 1902—1912. (d) Registration commenced in November 1911. (e) 1906—1912.
(f) 1907—1912. (g) 1905—1912. (h) 1903—1912.

XIII.—Holdings, Cultivation and Demand in fasli 1322.

Taluks.	Total holdings.						Cultivation including waste charged.				Miscellaneous revenue.	Total ryotwari demand.	Cesses.	Total demand of Land Revenue Ryotwar, Miscellaneous and Cesses.
	Dry.		Wet.		Total.		Dry.		Wet.					
	Extent.	Assessment.	Extent.	Assessment.	Extent.	Assessment.	Extent.	Assessment including water-rate.	Extent.	Assessment including second crop charge.				
(1)	(2)	(3)	(4)	(5)	(6)	(7)	(8)	(9)	(10)	(11)	(12)	(13)	(14)	(15)
SERMADEVI DIVISION.	ACS.	RS.	ACS.	RS.	ACS.	RS.	ACS.	RS.	ACS.	RS.	RS.	RS.	RS.	RS.
Ambasamudram ...	88,533	62,023	32,528	4,02,009	121,061	4,64,032	88,533	55,889	33,487	4,04,327	32,051	4,02,693	38,257	5,00,650
Nanguneri	243,437	1,16,810	32,706	2,67,343	270,232	3,84,153	243,437	1,20,181	32,066	2,68,081	31,274	3,90,343	33,174	4,23,417
TINNEVELLY DIVISION.														
Tinnevelly	107,981	49,033	29,074	3,42,878	137,035	3,91,911	107,981	51,730	29,670	3,48,160	23,200	3,70,260	32,631	4,08,807
Tenkasi	65,013	60,080	20,251	1,34,651	85,264	2,14,731	65,013	61,440	20,249	1,55,523	22,033	2,27,481	19,075	2,46,556
TUTICORIN DIVISION.														
Srivaikuntam ...	111,932	94,023	26,505	3,21,751	138,437	4,15,774	111,032	97,718	26,497	3,24,099	89,521	4,18,300	34,620	4,53,020
Tiruchendur ...	120,850	1,04,935	22,541	2,20,746	143,391	3,25,681	120,850	1,06,370	22,523	2,23,120	73,602	3,61,917	25,891	3,87,808
KOILPATTI DIVISION.														
Koilpatti	166,624	1,58,771	3,158	14,760	169,782	1,73,531	166,624	1,59,678	3,150	10,053	19,315	1,87,181	10,974	2,04,153
Sankaranainarkoil.	124,258	1,07,881	14,141	81,911	138,399	1,89,792	124,258	1,10,748	14,141	91,808	16,470	2,08,769	18,254	2,27,023
Huzur collections..	...	...	...	...	...	...	...	...	...	...	793	793	...	793
Total ...	1,028,628	7,43,056	181,508	18,07,149	1,310,221	25,50,205	1,028,628	7,63,766	1,81,333	18,53,671	2,42,319	26,33,448	2,19,076	28,52,519

NOTE.—The difference between column 13 and the sum of columns 9,11 and 12 is due to the fact that column 13 excludes the amount (Rs. 2,25,313) of fixed and seasonal remissions.

XIV.—Revenue payable by permanently settled estates in fasli 1322 (1912–13).

Serial number. (1)	Taluks and estates. (2)	Peishkush. (3)	Land-cess. (4)	Miscellaneous revenue. (5)	Total. (6)
		RS.	RS.	RS.	RS.
	SĒRMĀDĒVI DIVISION.				
	Ambāsamudram Taluk.				
1	Ūrkādu	12,927	1,339	2,530	24,804
2	Singampatti	8,008			
	Total ..	20,935	1,339	2,530	24,804
	Nānguneri Taluk.				
	Nil.				
	TINNEVELLY DIVISION.				
	Tinnevelly Taluk.				
	Nil.				
	Tenkāsi Taluk.				
3	Uttumalai	26,973	11,572	2,575	60,160
4	Surandai	668			
5	Chokkampatti	4,054			
6	Vairavankulam	4,180			
7	Nayināragaram	2,038			
8	Kunnakkudi	1,153			
9	Vallam	828			
10	Sillaraipuravu	342			
11	Kambaneri Pudukkudi ...	2,003			
12	Urmēnaazhgiyan	2,122			
13	Sivan Ādanūr	473			
14	Minnadiseri	213			
15	Kulaiyaneri	675			
16	Ānaikulam	291			
	Total ...	46,013	11,572	2,575	60,160
	TUTICORIN DIVISION.				
	Srivaikuntam Taluk.				
17	Pērūrani, two-thirds	1,459	1,673	7,390	12,664
18	Pērūrani, one-third	765			
19	Kārkurichi	1,377			
	Total ..	3,601	1,673	7,390	12,664
	KŌILPATTI DIVISION.				
	Kōilpatti Taluk.				
20	Ettaiyāpuram	77,985	21,121	1,143	1,[illegible]9,355
21	Manivāchchi ... ... -	1,832			
22	Kadambūr	3,748			

XIV.—Revenue payable by permanently settled estates in fasli 1322 (1912–13)—*cont.*

Serial number. (1)	Taluks and estates. (2)	Peishkush. (3)	Land-cess. (4)	Miscellaneous revenue. (5)	Total. (6)
	KŌILPATTI DIVISION—*cont.*	RS.	RS.	RS.	RS.
	Kōilpatti Taluk—cont.				
23	Āttankarai	2,245			
24	Mēla Māndai, two-thirds ...	960			
25	Do. one-third ...	453			
26	Kulattūr (North)	581			
27	Do. (East)	634			
28	Do. (South)	690			
29	Kādalkudi	916			
30	Mallisvarapuram	679			
31	Rāmaswāmipuram	236	21,121	1,143	1,29,355
32	Vadamalaipuram	916			
33	Subramaniyapuram	916			
34	Sundarapachchaiyāpuram ...	270			
35	Muttayapuram	191			
36	Arianāyakipuram	455			
37	Nāgalāpuram	6,401			
38	Pudūr	6,458			
39	Vēlāyudhapuram	470			
	Total ...	1,07,091	21,121	1,143	1,29,355
	Sankaranainarkōil Taluk.				
40	Sivagiri	54,580			
41	Gūdalūr	1,718			
42	Nelkattumseval...	1,232			
43	Talavankōttai	2,738			
44	Alagāpuri	669			
45	Naduvakkurichchi (Major Division).	1,220			
46	Naduvakkurichchi (Minor Division).	308			
47	Poignikuttālpperi Agilandapuram.	515			
48	Nochikulam	991	10,660	1,104	84,307
49	Tirumalainānyakkan Pudukkudi.	2,069			
50	Tiruvēttanallūr	1,645			
51	Viriruppu	458			
52	Kulasēkharamangalam ...	2,029			
53	Vellālankulam	429			
54	Ichchandā	557			
55	Panaiyūr	395			
56	Sivagnānapuram (West) ...	375			
57	Do. (East) ...	230			
58	Vāyali	400			
	Total ...	72,543	10,660	1,104	84,307
	District Total ...	2,50,183	46,865	14,742	3,11,290

XV.—Demand, Collection and Balance of Current Land Revenue and Cesses.

(In thousands of rupees.)

Taluks.	Demand.			Collected or written off.			Balance.		
	Fasli 1820	Fasli 1821.	Fasli 1822.	Fasli 1320.	Fasli 1321.	Fasli 1322.	Fasli 1320.	Fasli 1321.	Fasli 1322.
(1)	(2)	(3)	(4)	(5)	(6)	(7)	(8)	(9)	(10)
Sermādēvi Division.									
Ambāsamudram	521	530	530	521	530	528	...	...	2
Nānguneri	398	452	436	398	449	431	...	3	5
Tinnevelly Division.									
Tinnevelly	390	420	416	389	420	415	1	...	1
Tenkāsi	261	306	308	261	306	308	...	...	...
Tuticorin Division.									
Srivaikuntam	464	457	463	461	448	458	3	9	5
Tiruchendūr	275	313	390	273	312	387	2	1	3
Kōilpatti Division.									
Kōilpatti	277	337	346	275	337	346	2	...	...
Sankaranainārkōil	295	298	322	294	294	318	1	4	4
District Total ...	2881	3113	3211	2872	3096	3191	9	17	20

Note.—The omission of the figures of the previous faslis from this table has been necessitated by the redistribution of the administrative areas of the district effected in 1910.

XVI.—Remissions.

(In thousands of rupees.)

Taluks.	Waste remitted.								Other seasonal remissions (excluding fixed remissions).			
	Wet.				Dry.							
	Fasli 1320.	Fasli 1321.	Fasli 1322.	Total.	Fasli 1320.	Fasli 1321.	Fasli 1322.	Total.	Fasli 1320.	Fasli 1321.	Fasli 1322.	Total.
(1)	(2)	(3)	(4)	(5)	(6)	(7)	(8)	(9)	(10)	(11)	(12)	(13)
Sermadevi Division.												
Ambāsamudram	7	...	..	7	...	...	...	...	3	1	...	4
Nānguněri	12	1	1	14	...	...	...	...	11	1	2	14
Tinnevelly Division.												
Tinnevelly	8	1	...	4	..	...	...	...	25	3	...	27
Tenkāsi	1	...	...	1	...	..	...	...	14	1	...	15
Tuticorin Division.												
Srivaikuntam	3	1	...	4		...	...	...	4	1	...	5
Tiruchendur	6	2	...	8	...	...	...	...	6	2	1	9
Koilpatti Division.												
Koilpatti	1	1	...	2	...	...	...	...	1	1	...	2
Sankaranainārkoil	4	6	...	10	...	...	...	...	16	5	...	21
District Total ...	37	12	1	50	...	...	...	..	80	14	3	97

NOTE.—The omission from this table of the figures of the previous faslis has been necessitated by the redistribution of the administrative areas of the district effected in 1910.

XVII.—Land Improvement and Agriculturists' Loans.

Taluks.	Total amount advanced under the Land Improvement and Agriculturists Loans Acts in				Total recovered.
	Fasli 1320.	Fasli 1321.	Fasli 1322.	Total including outstanding balance at the beginning of fasli 1320.	
(1)	(2)	(3)	(4)	(5)	(6)
Sêrmâdêvi Division.					
Ambāsamudram	2,797	4,990	4,300	12,217	7,708
Nānguuēri	7,450	5,860	2,382	16,082	6,478
Tinnevelly Division.					
Tinnevelly	4,275	2,825	3,300	10,462	3,308
Tenkāsi	1,650	3,822	2,923	7,901	4,845
Tuticorin Division.					
Srīvaikuntam	1,700	2,125	1,325	5,202	2,035
Tiruchendūr	600	3,450	890	4,050	821
Kōilpatti Division.					
Kōilpatti	1,350	3,555	3,780	8,723	7,594
Sankaranainārkōil	3,282	8,280	9,811	21,430	13,577
Special Loans Deputy Collector	...	...	15,112	15,112	...
District Total ...	28,104	34,407	43,773	101,179	51,366

NOTE.—The omission of the figures of the faslis previous to fasli 1320 from this table has been necessitated by the redistribution of the administrative areas of the district effected in 1910.

XVIII.—Prices in seers per rupee.

Fasli.	Sērmādēvi Division.			Tinnevelly Division.		Tuticorin Division.				Kōilpatti Division.			
	Ambāsamudram. Taluk.	Nāngunēri Taluk.		Tinnevelly. Taluk.	Tenkāsi Taluk.	Srīvaikuntam Taluk.		Tiruchendūr Taluk.		Kōilpatti Taluk.		Sankaranainārkōil Taluk.	
	Ambāsamudram.	Nānguneri.	Rādhāpuram.	Tinnevelly.	Tenkāsi.	Srīvaikuntam.	Tuticorin.	Tiruchendūr.	Kulasekarapatnam.	Ōttappidāram.	Vilāttikulam.	Sankaranainārkōil.	District Average.
(1)	(2)	(3)	(4)	(5)	(6)	(7)	(8)	(9)	(10)	(11)	(12)	(18)	(14)
						Rice, second sort.							
1813	12·1	11·5	10·8	12·1	12·2	11·8	12·3	...	10·2	12·0	12·1	12·6	11·8
1814	11·9	11·0	10·0	11·8	11·3	10·4	11·7	...	9·8	11·8	10·9	11·0	10·1
1815	9·26	8·91	8·28	8·95	9·07	8·62	9·55	...	8·63	9·17	9·05	9·13	8·97
1816	9·4	9·0	7·5	8·8	9·3	8·9	8·8	...	8·1	8·5	8·4	9·2	8·7
1817	8·8	9·0	8·8	8·5	9·0	8·0	8·1	...	7·8	8·1	7·9	8·8	8·4
1818	7·7	8·1	5·9	8·0	8·1	8·2	8·2	...	7·4	8·0	8·0	7·9	7·8
1819	9·8	9·7	7·7	9·1	9·4	9·0	9·3	...	8·5	9·0	8·6	8·7	8·9
1820	9·8	8·5	8·0	9·1	8·8	8·4	9·6	8·5	8·0	9·3	9·1	8·0	8·7
1821	8·4	7·6	7·4	8·1	7·6	7·6	8·5	7·2	7·2	8·1	7·9	8·6	7·6
1822	7·4	7·2	6·7	7·2	7·6	6·5	7·8	6·9	6·9	7·4	7·2	8·2	7·3

Paddy, first sort.

1813	...	...	...	20·3	...	18·5	...	19·1	18·0	...	...	...	...	18·6	18·9
1814	...	...	...	...	..	17·8	..	17·5	17·0	...	...	...	...	16·2	17·1
1815	...	...	...	...	..	...	...	14·05	14·10	..	...	...	..	13·13	13·76
1816	...	...		...	..	..	..	15·0	12·9	...	...	..	...	13·4	13·8
1817	...	...	13·5	...	...	...	...	13·3	12·5	..	...	...	...	13·5	13·2
1818	...	...	...	...	..	...	...	12·6	12·2	...	...	...	...	11·5	12·1
1819	...	...	..	..	...	...	...	14·5	13·9	...	..	...	...	12·5	13·6
1820	..	...	...	...	...	...	...	13·9	14·0	...	...	...	...	12·6	13·5
1821	...	...	...	...	...	...	..	12·2	11·7	...	...	...	...	11·9	11·9
1822	...	...	...	...	...	...	...	11·4	11·8	...	...	...	...	10·9	11·4

Paddy, second sort.

1813	...	...	19·7	19·8	19·0	19·1	20·0	20·8	19·6	...	17·2	19·7	...	20·7	19·5
1814		...	19·2	18·0	16·9	17·5	18·0	18·5	18·0		16·9	17·4	...	18·0	17·8
1815	...	...	14·87	14·47	13·27	13·84	13·92	14·78	14·74	...	15·22	14·28	...	14·16	14·36
1816	...	...	15·4	14·4	11·8	14·4	14·6	16·6	13·8		14·1	13·9	...	14·9	14·4
1817	..	..	14·2	14·2	13·0	13·6	14·0	14·1	13·0	...	12·9	13·8	...	14·7	13·7
1818	..	...	13·2	12·1	9·7	13·0	12·5	13·2	12·9	...	11·8	13·0	...	12·4	12·4
1819	...	..	15·7	14·0	13·3	...	14·4	14·9	14·5	...	13·9	13·7	...	13·6	14·2
1820	...		15·1	13·9	13·7	...	13·8	14·6	14·7	13·3	12·9	13·9	...	13·7	14·0
1821	...	...	13·6	12·4	11·5	...	12·1	13·1	12·7	11·8	11·3	12·7	...	13·0	12·4
1822	...	...	12·4	11·6	10·3	...	11·9	12·0	12·2	11·2	10·6	11·3	10·9	12·4	11·5

Horsegram.

1813	...	...	20·7	21·3	...	20·9	20·8	19·3	...	...	...	..	...	22·2	20·9
1814	..	...	17·3	17·7		18·3	18·4	16·5	...	...	...	...	...	20·2	18·1
1815	...	...	11·82	12·79	19·08	12·39	12·11	11·87	...	...	...	...		11·75	13·19
1816	...	...	13·4	15·1	20·4	13·2	13·1	12·1	...	...	...	...		15·3	14·5
1817	...	..	16·8	13·2	...	16·9	16·7	15·0	...	...	...	...	...	14·0	17·1
1818	...		12·5	12·3		12·7	12·8	12·1	...	..	...	...		13·0	12·6
1819	...	...	10·7	9·8	...	10·8	11·6	10·6	..	...		...	...	10·0	10·6
1820	...	...	12·3	11·7		12·6	12·8	12·2	...	...	...	...	...	13·0	12·4
1821	...	...	14·5	14·7	...	15·0	14·0	13·1			...	...	...	13·6	14·2
1822	...	..	13·7	14·0	...	13·5	13·4	13·1	...	...	...	...	...	13·9	13·6

XVIII.—Prices in seers per rupee—*cont.*

Fasli.	Sērmādēvi Division.			Tinnevelly Division.		Tuticorin Division.				Kōilpatti Division.			District Average.
	Ambāsamudram Taluk.	Nāngunēri Taluk.		Tinnevelly Taluk.	Tenkāsi Taluk.	Srīvaikuntam Taluk.		Tiruchendūr Taluk.		Kōilpatti Taluk.		Sankaranainārkōil Taluk.	
	Ambāsamudram.	Nānguneri.	Rādhapuram.	Tinnevelly.	Tenkāsi.	Srīvaikuntam.	Tuticorin.	Tiruchendūr.	Kulasēkarapatnam.	Ottappidāram.	Villāttikulam.	Sankaranainārkōil.	District Average.
(1)	(2)	(3)	(4)	(5)	(6)	(7)	(8)	(9)	(10)	(11)	(12)	(13)	(14)
						Cholam.							
1813	...	...	...	21·1	21·9	...	...	...	...	22·2	...	22·7	22·0
1814	...	...	...	15·4	17·9	...	...	...	...	18·7	...	19·2	17·8
1815	...		...	13·81	12·68	...	...	...	...	...	...	13·64	13·38
1816	...	...	...	13·9	14·0	...	...		...	8·2	...	14·6	12·7
1817	...	...	...	15·4	15·0	...		...	...	11·0	...	15·4	14·2
1818	...	...	...	12·5	13·1	...	...	...	...	...	...	13·7	13·1
1819	...	...	...	14·3	15·5	...	...	...	...		...	15·8	15·0
1820	...	...	...	13·8	13·5			...	...	13·6	...	13·6	13·6
1821	...	...	...	12·6	14·8	...	...	...	...	12·7	...	13·0	12·8
1822	...	...	...	11·9	12·3	...	...	...	...	...	...	12·7	12·3

Year															
								Oambu.							
1813	...	...	...	..	...	16·3	...	..	16·8	..	...	17·2	17·9	...	17·1
1814	...		...	...	.	14·7	...	...	15·8	...	...	16·7	15·8	19·2	16·8
1815	...	...	...	...	...	11·34	...		11·95	...	...	14·68	12·35	18·76	12·82
1816	...	...	...	...	...	11·7	...	...	12·3	...	...	12·1	13·8	16·1	18·2
1817	...	...	...	...	...	12·4	..	...	12·2	...	...	12·9	15·7	15·8	18·8
1818	...	...	...	...	...	10·7	...	...	11·4	...	...	11·8	14·2	...	12·0
1819	...	...	12·2	...	...	...	...	...	10·9	..	...	11·7	12·7	11·8	11·8
1820	...	...	...	...	...	11·5	...	...	11·0	...	...	11·9	12·6	14·4	12·3
1821	...	...	...	...	...	11·5	...	...	11·0	...	...	12·2	12·2	15·0	12·4
1822	...	...	...	...	...	11·1	...	...	11·0	...	..	11·9	18·0	14·1	12·2
								Varagu (unhusked).							
1813	...	...	...	.	45·5	...	.	...	...	...	...	...	...	...	45·5
1814	...	...	...	...	25·9	...	...	...	..	...	...	...	...	...	25·9
1815	...	...	...	...	25·60	...	...	...	..	...	...	...	...	...	25·60
1816	...	...	..	...	22·8	...	...	...	.	..	...	...	...	12·9	17·9
1817	...	...	...	...	21·8	...	..	.	...	...	...	...	...	...	21·8
1818	...	...	...	...	...	...	...	...	...	...	...	...	...	...	...
1819	...	...	...	...	...	...	...	...	...	...	...	...	...	..	...
1820	...	...	...	...	...	...	...	...	...	...	...	...	...	...	..
1821	..	...	...	...	...	...	...	...	...	...	...	...	...	...	...
1822	...	...	...	...	...	...	...	...	...	...	...	...	...	...	...
								Ragi.							
1813	...	...	...	...	...	...	..	...	...	...	...	...	...	...	...
1814	...	..	...	...	...	...	...	...	...	...	...	...	...	...	...
1815	...	...	...	...	...	...	...	...	...	...	...	...	...	...	...
1816	...	...	...	...	...	...	...	...	...	...	...	...	...	...	...
1817	...	...	...	...	...	...	...	...	...	...	..	...	...	...	...
1818	...	...	...	...	...	...	...	...	...	...	...	...	...	...	...
1819	...	...	...	...	...	...	...	...	...	...	...	...	...	...	...
1820	...	...	...	...	...	18·7	...	...	...	...	...	...	...	...	18·7
1821	...	...	...	...	...	18·9	...	...	...	...	...	...	...	15·8	14·6
1822	...	...	...	...	...	12·5	...	...	...	...	...	...	...	14·1	18·8

XVIII.—Prices in seers per rupee—*cont.*

Fasli.	Sērmādēvi Division.			Tinnevelly Division.		Tuticorin Division.				Kōilpatti Division.			District Average.
	Ambāsamudram Taluk.	Nānguneri Taluk.		Tinnevelly Taluk.	Tenkāsi Taluk.	Srīvaikuntam Taluk.		Tiruchendūr Taluk.		Kōilpatti Taluk.		Sankaranainārkōil Taluk.	
	Ambāsamudram.	Nānguneri.	Rādhāpuram.	Tinnevelly.	Tenkāsi.	Srīvaikuntam.	Tuticorin.	Tiruchendūr.	Kulasekarapatnam.	Ōttappidāram.	Vilāttikulam.	Sankaranainārkōil.	District Average.
(1)	(2)	(3)	(4)	(5)	(6)	(7)	(8)	(9)	(10)	(11)	(12)	(13)	(14)
						Salt.							
1313	16·7	16·0	16·2	17·6	16·5	16·7	17·3	...	17·2	16·7	15·5	15·8	16·6
1314	16·2	15·8	16·4	17·0	15·6	16·9	17·1	...	18·4	16·8	15·7	14·1	16·4
1315	18·23	18·90	20·53	19·36	17·70	19·70	20·25	...	21·24	19·78	17·64	17·20	19·15
1316	18·8	19·9	20·4	20·1	19·3	21·3	22·1	...	22·7	21·2	18·8	19·4	20·4
1317	23·6	26·1	23·8	27·5	23·1	25·6	26·1	...	27·6	28·0	22·0	23·9	25·2
1318	22·9	25·8	25·9	27·6	22·9	26·5	26·4	...	24·2	29·0	23·6	24·0	25·3
1319	24·0	28·6	26·3	27·6	23·4	25·9	25·9	...	25·4	25·4	23·6	24·3	25·0
1320	24·0	23·9	25·9	28·7	23·3	26·0	23·7	26·3	26·4	26·3	23·2	23·6	25·1
1321	24·0	24·4	25·9	27·3	23·8	26·5	24·0	24·9	27·3	27·6	24·1	22·4	25·1
1322	23·4	24·3	26·5	26·2	22·6	26·4	23·7	26·2	24·7	27·6	23·7	22·9	24·8

XIX.—Income-tax.

(Part IV. "Other sources" only.)

Taluks.	Rs. 1,000 to Rs. 1,500.		Rs. 1,500 to Rs. 2,000.		Above Rs. 2,000.		Total.		Incidence of tax.		Objection petitions.	
	Number of assessees.	Amount of tax.	Number of assessees.	Amount of tax.	Number of assessees.	Amount of tax.	Number of assessees.	Amount of tax.	Per head of assessees.	Per head of population.	Number.	Percentage of these wholly or partially successful.
(1)	(2)	(3)	(4)	(5)	(6)	(7)	(8)	(9)	(10)	(11)	(12)	(13)
Sêrmâdêvi Division.		RS.		RS.		RS.		RS.	RS. A. P.	A. P.		
Ambâsamudram. 1910-11	68	1,632	26	994	42	7,531	136	10,157	74 10 11	0 10	39	12·8
1911-12	69	1,692	29	1,099	43	8,028	141	10,819	76 11 8	0 11	39	12·82
1912-13	71	1,644	46	1,743	49	8,519	166	11,906	71 11 6	1 0	82	9·7
Nânguneri ... 1910-11	32	720	6	238	6	609	44	1,567	35 9 10	0 1	7	14·2
1911-12	25	580	5	196	9	865	39	1,661	42 9 5	0 2	16	12·50
1912-13	24	568	6	224	10	1,097	40	1,889	47 3 7	0 2	18	15·3
Tinnevelly Division.												
Tinnevelly ... 1910-11	131	2,988	61	2,380	121	16,650	318	22,018	70 5 10	1 8	53	18·8
1911-12	121	2,780	58	2,240	131	18,059	310	23,079	74 7 2	1 9	33	21·21
1912-13	135	3,185	58	2,247	116	15,880	309	21,312	68 15 6	1 7	37	29·7
Tenkâsi 1910-11	37	870	19	714	11	1,579	67	3,163	47 3 4	0 8	14	7·1
1911-12	35	812	20	735	15	1,292	70	2,839	40 8 11	0 3	20	35·00
1912-13	36	848	17	630	10	1,111	63	2,589	41 1 6	0 8	10	10·00

XIX.—Income-tax.

(Part IV. "Other sources" only—*cont.*)

Taluk.	Rs. 1,000 to 1,500.		Rs. 1,500 to 2,000.		Above Rs. 2,000.		Total.		Incidence of tax.		Objection petitions.	
	Number of assessees.	Amount of tax.	Number of assessees.	Amount of tax.	Number of assessees.	Amount of tax.	Number of assessees.	Amount of tax.	Per head of assessees.	Per head of population.	Number.	Percentage of those wholly or partially successful.
(1)	(2)	(3)	(4)	(5)	(6)	(7)	(8)	(9)	(10)	(11)	(12)	(13)
TUTICORIN DIVISION.		RS.		RS.		RS.		RS.	RS. A. P.	A. P.		
Srivaikuntam ... 1910-11	105	2,390	55	2,163	125	25,196	285	29,739	104 5 6	2 4	58	23·4
1911-12	112	2,584	68	2,446	147	29,352	327	34,382	105 2 4	2 9	50	26·00
1912-13	106	2,879	79	3,027	136	28,835	321	33,741	105 1 9	2 8	60	26·6
Tiruchendūr ... 1910-11	43	1,020	26	1,022	28	3,941	97	5,983	61 10 10	0 5	45	22·2
1911-12	26	832	23	875	39	3,767	88	5,474	62 3 8	0 5	29	24·13
1912-13	43	974	24	814	32	4,461	99	6,249	63 0 4	0 6	48	29·1
KŌILPATTI DIVISION.												
Kōilpatti .. 1910-11	115	2,716	74	3,046	70	9,593	259	15,355	59 4 6	0 9	66	27·3
1911-12	112	2,640	73	2,775	93	10,355	278	15,770	56 11 8	0 9	74	28·37
1912-13	117	2,635	86	3,359	18	3,856	221	9,850	44 9 1	0 6	88	19·2
Sankaranainārkōil. 1910-11	15	372	20	784	19	2,209	54	3,365	62 5 7	0 3	29	6·8
1911-12	18	432	23	917	30	2,811	71	4,160	58 9 6	0 3	36	30·55
1912-13	20	463	30	1,207	82	9,451	132	11,121	84 2 9	0 9	36	13·8
District Total ... 1910-11	546	12,698	287	11,341	422	67,308	1,255	91,347	72 12 6	0 11	311	19·3
1911-12	518	12,352	299	11,283	507	74,549	1,324	98,184	74 2 6	0 11	297	24·57
1912-13	552	12,696	346	13,251	453	72,710	1,351	98,657	73 0 4	0 11	374	19·8

NOTE.—The omission from this table of the figures of the two years 1908-1909 and 1909-1910 has been necessitated by the redistribution of the administrative areas of the district effected in 1910.

XX.—Abkāri and Opium.

(1)	1910–11. (2)	1911–12. (3)	1912–13. (4)
Country spirits.			
Number of retail shops licensed	312	313	313
Issues in imperial proof gallons	53,033	47,943	49,109
Number of persons per retail shop	5,741	5,721	5,721
Gross receipts from duty ... ... Rs.	3,04,074	3,06,069	3,07,281
Do. rentals ... ... ,,	1,39,347	1,68,995	1,63,819
Toddy.			
Number of retail shops licensed	624	625	618
Number of persons per shop	2,871	2,865	2,897
Gross receipts from tree-tax ... ... Rs.	1,75,409	1,68,353	2,07,007
Do. rentals ... ... ,,	1,82,289	1,60,115	1,65,200
Ganja, Bhang, etc.			
Number of retail shops licensed	26	29	28
Quantity sold in seers	1,909	1,668	2,131
Number of persons per shop	94,275	94,243	99,478
Gross receipts from duty ... ... Rs.	3,760	10,647	12,833
Do. rentals ... ... ,,	9,516	9,888	11,005
Opium.			
Number of retail shops licensed	13	13	12
Quantity sold in seers	269	351	332
Number of persons per shop	137,787	137,740	149,218
Gross receipts from duty ... ... Rs.	5,545	7,196	8,230
Do. rentals ... ... ,,	6,100	6,272	5,805

NOTE.—The omission of the figures of the previous years has been necessitated by the redistribution of the administrative areas of the district effected in 1910.

XXI.—Revenue Receipts.

—	1910-11.	1911-12.	1912-13.
(1)	(2)	(3)	(4)
	RS.	RS.	RS.
Land Revenue	28,32,907	27,07,410	29,38,675
Stamps	6,63,203	6,47,939	7,21,456
Excise	8,29,271	8,43,789	8,78,391
Incometax including penalties ...	1,54,943	1,60,686	1,65,037
Forests	1,10,854	92,497	1,03,964
Registration *	1,67,831	1,62,316	1,78,124
Opium	11,645	13,468	14,035
Salt	17,32,568	17,67,033	16,77,805
Customs	5,41,857	6,07,355	6,24,319

* The figures under "Registration" are for the calendar years and for the Registration District of Tinnevelly.

NOTE.—The omission of the figures of the previous years has been necessitated by the reconstitution of the district effected in 1910.

XXII.—Sea-borne Trade—Total Trade in each port.

Names of ports.	Imports.					Exports				
	1908-09.	1909-10.	1910-11.	1911-12.	1912-13.	1908-09.	1909-10.	1910-11.	1911-12.	1912-13.
(1)	(2)	(3)	(4)	(5)	(6)	(7)	(8)	(9)	(10)	(11)
TUTICORIN.	RS.	RS.	RS.	RS.	RS.	RS.	RS.	RS.	RS.	RS.
Merchandise	1,57,43,533	2,18,43,164	2,11,77,653	2,06,78,840	2,17,16,133	4,09,64,156	4,74,62,311	5,36,56,848	5,68,04,150	6,45,39,859
Treasure	1,00,262	69	15,23,235	11,37,095	14,684	40,79,255	55,20,153	71,59,430	44,15,480	37,68,104
Total ...	1,58,43,795	2,18,43,233	2,27,00,888	2,18,15,935	2,17,30,817	4,50,43,411	5,29,82,464	6,08,16,278	6,12,19,630	6,83,07,463
KULASÊKHARAPATNAM.										
Merchandise	7,53,015	8,25,519	10,55,082	11,36,229	7,67,958	6,39,081	7,40,869	9,16,883	7,88,295	8,52,072
Treasure	Nil.	34,500	8,17,000	1,92,000	1,92,000	Nil.	Nil.	15,000	6,000	1,000
Total ...	7,53,015	8,60,019	18,72,082	13,28,229	9,59,958	6,39,081	7,40,869	9,31,883	7,94,295	8,53,072
KĀYALPATNAM.										
Merchandise	2,12,699	3,58,704	8,31,393	3,62,867	2,72,655	5,08,447	5,20,221	5,93,560	6,68,744	6,70,863
Treasure	Nil.	Nil.	13,000	2,000	1,000	Nil.	Nil.	Nil.	Nil.	Nil.
Total ...	2,12,699	3,58,704	8,44,393	3,64,867	2,73,655	5,08,447	5,20,221	5,93,560	6,68,744	6,70,863

XXII-A.—Sea-borne Trade—Chief Imports and Exports in selected ports.

(Average of the five years ending 1912-18.)

Name of port. (1)	Imports. Articles. (2)		Imports. Quantity. (3)	Imports. Value. (4)	Exports. Articles. (5)		Exports. Quantity. (6)	Exports. Value. (7)
				RS.				RS.
	Apparel	val.	...	1,48,967	Animals living	No.	887,278	14,49,248
	Chemicals	"	...	1,05,984	Drugs and medicines (mainly senna)	val.	...	6,31,801
	Coal, coke and patent fuel ...	Tons.	7,864	1,01,802				
	Dyeing and tanning substances—				Dyeing and tanning substances—			
	Alizarine	lb.	742,947	5,25,907	Turmeric	cwt.	7,308	82,815
	Aniline...	"	75,982	64,917	Fibre for brushes and brooms (Palmyra fibre)	"	45,551	724,067
	Other sorts	val.	...	85,661	Fish—			
	Hardware and cutlery ...	"	...	2,12,958	Fish, dry, unsalted	cwt.	81,928	2,38,966
	Grain and pulse—				Fish, dry, salted	"	115,060	12,02,647
	Gram	cwt.	205,283	9,58,063	Coffee	"	10,359	4,92,378
	Jawar and bajra	"	17,865	90,261	Fruits and vegetables—			
	Pulse	"	810,228	16,00,709	Vegetables, fresh (mainly onions)	val.	...	8,37,284
	Rice in the husk	"	852,188	11,83,027	Fruits, dried	cwt.	21,352	89,889
	Rice not in the husk... ...	"	156,850	7,78,200	Grain and Pulse —			
	Wheat flour	"	19,182	1,61,409	Gram	cwt.	13,056	59,843
	Other sorts	"	14,084	82,759	Pulse	"	18,183	71,856
	Hides and skins, raw—				Rice in the husk	"	202,510	5,53,638
	Hides, raw	cwt.	651	23,078	Rice not in the husk	"	947,064	63,15,372
	Skins, raw	"	6,260	2,76,251	Other sorts	"	4,218	24,977
	Jewellery	val.	...	67,918				

Tuticorin.

Article	Unit	Quantity	Value
Leather—			
Hides dressed or tanned ...	cwt.	1,246	1,07,623
Other kinds of leather ...	val.	...	63,094
Machinery and Mill work ...	„	...	8,54,387
Matches	„	...	1,31,425
Metals—			
Copper...	cwt.	8,001	4,19,435
Iron and steel	tons.	3,864	5,99,366
Lead	cwt.	3,178	45,279
Oils—			
Mineral Kerosine	galls.	2,078,815	8,06,402
Other kinds	„	89,475	38,796
Castor	„	46,466	55,987
Other sorts of oils	„	2,871	5,868
Provisions and oilmen's stores	val.	...	2,58,731
Salt	tons.	16,217	5,38,819
Seeds—			
Essential	cwt.	31,944	6,06,909
Mustard	„	7,018	59,684
Til or gingelly	„	10,913	1,02,090
Other sorts	„	5,399	1,03,523
Spices—			
Betel-nuts	lb.	9,211,481	16,11,206
Other sorts	„	115,438	41,204
Sugar—			
16 Dutch standard and above	cwt.	67,630	7,44,342
Other sorts	„	591	18,269
Textiles—			
Cotton, raw	cwt.	12,799	5,36,219
Cotton, twist and yarn ...	lb.	2,815,223	20,42,901
Manures—			
Bones	tons.	2,420	1,23,217
Oil cakes	cwt.	487,705	22,39,253
Rubber, raw	„	1,573	7,06,539
Seeds—			
Coriander	cwt.	10,697	94,860
Cotton	„	34,686	1,84,715
Other sorts	„	5,108	49,176
Spices—			
Cardamoms	lb.	666,992	9,13,658
Chillies	„	5,885,512	10,10,573
Other sorts	„	819,108	65,122
Sugar	cwt.	15,420	1,09,489
Tea, black	lb.	10,133,391	62,79,046
Tea, green	„	279,691	1,74,805
Textiles—			
Cotton, raw	cwt.	503,425	1,98,81,995
Cotton, twist and yarn ...	lb.	4,857,204	25,24,179
Cotton Piece goods—			
Coloured printed, etc. ...	yds.	7,206,733	23,97,982
Jute gunny bags	No.	373,187	74,872
Tobacco manufactured ...	lb.	84,077	1,22,020
Articles exported by post ...	val.	...	15,39,892
All other articles	„	...	14,70,200
Total ...		...	5,26,85,364
Treasure ...		...	49,88,485
Grand Total ...		...	5,76,73,849

XXII-A.—Sea-borne Trade—Chief Imports and Exports in selected ports—*cont.*

(Average of the five years ending 1912-13.)

Name of port. (1)	Imports. Articles. (2)		Quantity. (3)	Value. (4)	Exports. Articles (5)	Quantity. (6)	Value. (7)
Tuticorin—*cont.*				RS.			RS.
	Cotton Piece goods—						
	Grey	yds.	5,071,796	7,76,852			
	White	„	881,424	61,737			
	Coloured, etc., ...	„	148,156	87,838			
	Other sorts of manufactures,	val.	...	20,242			
	Jute—						
	Gunny bags	No.	2,996,933	5,46,667			
	Other sorts	val.	...	83,266			
	Silk, raw	lb.	28,464	1,54,814			
	Wood and timber—						
	Teakwood	c. ton .	895	78,420			
	Other sorts	val.	...	1,16,046			
	Articles imported by post ...	„	...	4,93,481			
	All other articles	„	...	16,03,122			
	Total ...		...	2,02,31,864			
	Treasure ...		...	5,55,069			
	Grand Total ...		...	2,07,86,938			

Port	Articles	Unit	Quantity	Value	Articles	Unit	Quantity	Value
Kāyalpatnam.	Grain and pulse—				Salt	tons.	16,157	5,86,582
	Rice in the husk	cwt.	41,162	1,58,496	Sugar	cwt.	9,194	40,544
	Rice not in the husk ...	„	2,117	11,891	All other articles	val.	...	15,241
	Spices—betel-nuts	lb.	164,285	21,083	Total ...		...	5,92,367
	Textiles—Jute gunny bags.	No.	241,415	47,661				
	All other articles	val.	...	68,582	Treasure ...		...	
	Total ...		...	3,07,663	Grand Total ...		...	5,92,367
	Treasure ...		...	3,200				
	Grand Total ...		...	3,10,863				
Kulasekarapatnam.					Mats and matting ...	...Sq. yd.	4,033,700	48,483
	Grain and pulse—				Sugar—			
	Pulse	cwt.	2,968	14,596	16 Dutch standard and			
	Rice in the husk	„	110,869	4,12,418	above	cwt.	85,354	4,07,944
	Rice not in the husk ...	„	2,862	16,614	15 Dutch standard and below	„	74,358	2,04,619
	Fish, dry, salted	„	8,721	65,828	Textiles—			
	Seeds	„	3,363	18,038	Jute gunny bags	No	91,626	18.166
	Spices—				All other articles	val.	...	1,18,228
	Betel-nuts	lb.	532,579	1,11,125	Total ..		...	7,87,440
	Sugar—							
	15 Dutch standard and below	cwt.	14,076	64,490	Treasure ...		.	4,400
	Textiles—							
	Jute gunny bags	No.	47,736	10,381				
	All other articles	val.	...	2,04,070	Grand Total ...		...	7,91,840
	Total ...		...	9,07,560				
	Treasure ...			1,47,100				
	Grand Total ...		...	10,54,660				

XXIII.—Income and Expenditure of Local Boards in 1912-13.

(1)	District Board. (2)	Taluk Boards including unions in them. Sermadevi. (3)	Tinnevelly. (4)	Tuticorin. (5)	Koilpatti. (6)	Total (7)
	RS.	RS.	RS.	RS.	RS.	RS.
REVENUE AND RECEIPTS.						
Land Revenue—						
House-tax	...	23,943	10,298	19,276	17,754	71,271
Rents, etc., of fisheries	...	3,768	4,045	7,286	662	15,761
Miscellaneous	...	...	.	...	...	...
Local rates—						
Cess on Land	1,16,842	30,735	26,661	25,836	33,609	2,33,683
Railway Cess	62,390	...	...	...	...	62,390
Interest -						
On Government Securities, etc.	21,305	519	121	107	52	22,104
Law and Justice—Courts of Law—						
Fines under Police and other Acts	...	736	421	942	1,020	3,119
Education—						
School fees	...	447	520	298	1,568	2,833
Contributions	393	4,643	5,417	6,720	3,856	20,029
Other receipts	...	4	101	...	18	123
Medical—						
Hospital receipts	...	1	...	...	...	1
Contributions	1,931	644	239	403	6,788	10,105
Other receipts	16	438	372	1,012	743	2,481
Minor departments—						
Veterinary, etc., receipts	...	...	...	...	...	...
Miscellaneous—						
Choultry receipts	...	39,833	6,496	5,490	510	52,329
Market and slaughter house receipts	...	2,521	7,662	4,880	7,040	22,103
Contributions	...	...	348	...	132	480
Other receipts	3,286	1,907	1,137	1,599	1,601	9,530
Railways—						
Net receipts	...	...	...	...	...	...
Civil works—						
Ferry receipts	650	...	...	...	...	650
Tolls	88,905	...	...	...	...	88,905
Contributions—						
Contribution from Government	58,580	9,873	7,295	15,509	11,916	1,03,173
Other contributions	17,666	1,822	1,945	1,830	2,477	25,740
Debt, deposit and advances	50,657	680	2,024	698	906	54,964
Total Receipts ...	4,23,621	1,22,514	75,003	91,976	89,661	8,01,774
EXPENDITURE.						
Refunds—						
Land Revenue and local rates	..	4	36	...	3	43
Interest—						
On loans, etc.	...	..	...	...	...	...
General Administration—						
General establishment of Local Funds	10,131	5,405	3,389	5,070	4,860	28,855
Other expenditure	378	771	387	743	604	2,883
Education—						
Secondary schools		582	362	687	...	1,631
Elementary schools	...	15,264	10,459	9,072	14,692	49,487
Other schools	4,055	...	...	...	...	4,055
Other expenditure	1,000	..	...	...	...	1,000
Medical—						
Hospitals and dispensaries	4,276	12,509	7,574	1,961	10,285	46,605
Vaccination	...	1,491	1,344	1,489	1,679	6,003
Sanitation	...	11,868	5,495	11,361	7,939	36,653
Plague	3,227	...	...	...	...	3,227
Other epidemics	...	553	199	133	137	1,022
Other expenditure	1,675	...	...	...	...	1,675
Minor departments—						
Public exhibition and fairs	...	...	...	...	...	...
Veterinary and other charges	...	...	...	...	...	...

XXIII.—Income and Expenditure of Local Boards in 1912-13—*cont.*

		Taluk Boards including unions in them.				
—	District Board.	Sērmādēvi.	Tinnevelly.	Tuticorin.	Koilpatti.	Total.
(1)	(2)	(3)	(4)	(5)	(6)	(7)
	RS.	RS.	RS.	RS.	RS.	RS.
EXPENDITURE—*cont.*						
Superannuation, etc.—						
Pensions, Gratuities, etc.	3,589	256	168	213	273	4,409
Stationery and Printing—						
Stationery supplied from Central Stores ...	...	...	...	...	...	...
Printing work at Government and private presses.	1,013	326	422	908	434	3,103
Miscellaneous—						
Markets and slaughter houses	...	71	604	398	814	1,887
Choultries	...	23,770	6,109	3,193	752	33,824
Lighting	...	3,476	1,310	2,920	2,058	9,764
Other expenditure	428	257	567	203	775	2,230
Railways—						
Construction of railways	...	...	...	...	...	...
Other expenditure	...	...	...	...	...	...
Civil works—						
Civil buildings	2,833	4,812	3,080	5,636	3,778	19,669
Communications	2,65,070	33,989	18,412	19,609	20,228	3,56,908
Sanitary works and other works of public improvements.	...	8,896	9,486	11,169	14,750	44,301
Establishment, tools and plant	30,889	4,310	2,257	2,559	4,526	44,541
Contributions	...	...	87	...	...	87
Other expenditure	163	275	503	5	167	1,103
Debt, deposit and advances	1,32,445	998	3,651	494	928	1,37,514
Total Expenditure ...	4,51,762	1,20,411	73,901	67,823	98,672	8,41,569

XXIV.—Income and Expenditure of Municipalities in 1912–13.

(1)	Municipality. Palamcottah. (2)	Tinnevelly. (3)	Tuticorin. (4)
	RS.	RS.	RS.
Opening balance	7,106	20,965	3,143
RECEIPTS.			
Tax on buildings and lands	18,821	31,140	43,166
Water and drainage tax on buildings and lands.	...	...	...
Tax on vehicles with springs, animals and carts.	8,187	8,998	4,571
Tax on arts	3,563	6,254	9,991
Tolls	13,283	11,540	17,031
Tax on private menial and domestic servants.	...	...	...
Realizations under Special Acts	149	139	132
Rent of lands, buildings, etc., and sale-proceeds of lands, etc.	1,747	1,087	422
Conservancy receipts	2,191	1,981	263
Fees and Revenue from—			
Educational Institutions	84	...	...
Medical Institutions	319	88	500
Markets and slaughter houses	5,328	3,922	716
License fees	878	1,696	3,417
Other fees	188	60	226
Fines under Municipal and other Acts ...	1,085	1,608	2,020
Interest on investments and premium on loans.	2,853	1,757	1,168
Grants and contributions from—			
Government	83,121	1,16,651	2,223
Local Boards	1,896	1,431	75
Other sources	..	1,014	...
Recoveries for services rendered to private individuals.	4,689	7,590	5,911
Miscellaneous	359	1,585	1,099
Sale-proceeds of Government securities and realizations of Sinking Fund.	...	...	...
Loans	...	...	...
Advances recovered	81	9,739	1,039
Total Receipts ...	98,667	2,08,180	93,970
Total including balance ...	1,05,773	2,29,145	97,113

XXIV.—Income and Expenditure of Municipalities in 1912–13—*cont.*

—	Municipality.		
	Palamcottah.	Tinnevelly.	Tuticorin.
(1)	(2)	(3)	(4)
Expenditure.	RS.	RS.	RS.
Grant 1—			
Communications	9,426	14,185	13,146
Buildings	5,492	19,084	1,426
Miscellaneous Public Improvements ...	1,357	11,211	900
Drainage	152	3,481	121
Water-supply	413	2,016	8,868
Establishment	914	1,044	978
Tools and plant and other stores ...	...	102	169
Contributions for public works ...	...	100	...
Grant 2—			
Education	4,744	5,375	6,104
Grant 3—			
Hospitals and Dispensaries	11,463	9,222	10,845
Vaccination	489	452	275
Registration of births and deaths ...	319	375	175
Conservancy, road cleaning and road watering.	15,042	24,857	[illegible]5,324
Contributions	61	86	188
Plague charges	32	97	1,042
Veterinary charges	...	...	...
Cholera charges	348	...	2,093
Grant 4—			
Lighting	4,795	6,451	4,535
Markets and Slaughter houses ...	558	5[illegible]5	81
Choultries and Travellers' Bungalows.	252	...	87
Avenues	257	98	60
Public garden, survey of land, fire, pounds and other charges.	1,428	8,717	2,699
Grant 5—			
Supervision and management	5,465	4,422	6,852
Repayment of debt	...	...	2,830
Interest on debt	...	...	1,401
Discount on investment	...	...	...
Advances	40	203	3,480
Refunds	34	20	175
Investments	...	1,600	...
Total Expenditure ...	63,076	1,08,653	88,304
Closing balance ...	42,697	1,20,492	8,809
Total including balance ...	1,05,773	2,29,145	97,113

XXV.—Education in 1911.

Taluks.	Number of literates.		Literates per thousand of population.		Literates in English.	
	Males.	Females.	Males.	Females.	Males.	Females.
(1)	(2)	(3)	(4)	(5)	(6)	(7)
Sērmādēvi Division.						
Ambāsamudram	22,851	2,203	249	22	1,711	58
Nānguuēri	18,992	2,853	198	26	744	115
Tinnevelly Division.						
Tinnevelly	30,101	3,986	298	36	4,692	409
Tenkāsi	18,455	1,810	192	13	691	94
Tuticorin Division.						
Srivaikuntam	26,349	3,329	272	36	2,541	382
Tiruchendūr	28,154	7,564	274	68	1,165	362
Kōilpatti Division.						
Kōilpatti	35,835	1,573	217	9	920	62
Sankaranainārkōil	17,465	748	153	6	515	36
District Total ...	198,202	24,066	229	26	12,979	1,518
Hindus	157,650	9,624	215	12	9,134	118
Mussalmans	13,971	669	298	11	334	1
Christians	26,561	3,772	315	150	3,499	1,399
Others	20	1	741	200	12	...

XXVI.—Schools and Scholars in 1912–13.

Class of institutions.	Number of institutions.						Number of scholars.		
	Government.	Local Fund.	Municipal.	Aided.	Unaided.	Total.	Males.	Females.	Total.
(1)	(2)	(3)	(4)	(5)	(6)	(7)	(8)	(9)	(10)
Public.									
Arts Colleges ...	...	.	..	3	...	3	232	7	239
Professional Colleges.	...	...	...	...	...	...	...	..	..
a Secondary schools for boys.	...	...	...	27	1	28	6,798	19	6,817
a Secondary schools for girls.	..	...	...	7	...	7	9	893	902
b Higher Elementary schools for boys.	..	1	...	7	3	11	1,234	135	1,369
b Higher Elementary schools for girls.	...	...	1	14	...	15	33	1,881	1,914
c Lower Elementary schools for boys.	1	139	5	1,116	209	1,470	56,479	7,884	64,363
c Lower Elementary schools for girls.	1	7	2	103	6	119	270	6,064	6,334
Training schools for masters.	1	2	...	2	...	5	249		249
Training schools for mistresses.	...	...	...	2	...	2	...	50	50
Other special schools.	...	...	...	5	...	5	79	87	166
Total ...	3	149	8	1,286	219	1,665	65,383	17,020	82,403
Private.									
Advanced	...	...	.	...	...	26	327	225	552
Elementary	...	...	...	..	...	304	7,139	1,148	8,287
Total ...	...	...	..	.	...	330	7,466	1,373	8,839
Grand Total .	3	149	8	1,286	219	1,995	72,849	18,393	91,242

(*a*) Includes European high and middle schools.
(*b*) Relates to Elementary schools with standards above the fourth.
(*c*) Relates to Elementary schools with standards up to and including the fourth. Elementary schools with standards below the fourth and European Primary schools.

XXVII.—Expenditure on Schools in 1912-13.

Nature of schools.	Expenditure on all classes of schools.		Colleges.		Secondary schools.		Higher elementary schools.		Lower elementary schools.		Training schools.		Technical and Industrial schools.	
	Total.	Net.	Total expenditure.	Net expenditure.	Total expenditure.	Net expenditure.	Total expenditure.	Net expenditure.	Total expenditure.	Net expenditure	Total expenditure.	Net expenditure.	Total expenditure.	Net expenditure.
(1)	(2)	(3)	(4)	(5)	(6)	(7)	(8)	(9)	(10)	(11)	(12)	(13)	(14)	(15)
	Rs.	Rs.	Rs.	Rs.	Rs.	Rs.	Rs.	Rs.	Rs.	Rs.	Rs.	Rs.	Rs.	Rs.
Government ...	13,668	13,454	..	...	...	...	...	...	1,668	1,455	12,000	11,999	..	...
Local Fund ...	53,161	50,198	...	...	...	...	1,410	1,141	47,954	45,260	8,797	3,797	...	...
Municipal ...	7,419	6,829	...	...	...	...	1,258	1,258	6,161	5,671	...	..		...
Aided ...	5,67,607	2,13,994	22,821	—1,559	2,82,684	60,382	32,152	21,408	2,30,283	1,05,920	37,607	19,143	12,060	8,750
Unaided ...	19,101	12,858	..	...	1,560	960	1,626	964	16,015	10,934	...	...	...	...
Private ...	36,548	20,078	..	...	17,524	15,843	...	...	19,024	5,680	...	...	...	...
District Total ..	6,97,504	3,18,306	22,821	—1,559	2,51,768	76,635	36,346	24,771	3,21,105	1,74,770	53,404	34,939	12,060	8,750
Receipts (taken in abatement of charges in working out net expenditure) from—														
Provincial Funds	...	1,82,021	...	2,734	...	56,246	...	6,755	...	94,512	...	18,464	...	3,810
Local Funds ...	...	1,631	...	...	...	1,631		...	...	...	...	...	...	...
Municipal Funds	...	8,988	...	...	...	...	...	1,351	...	7,637	..	...	...	...
School fees ...	..	1,76,599	...	21,646	...	1,12,598	...	1,982	...	40,378	...	...	...	...
Subscriptions.	...	6,148	...	...	...	2,473	...	577	...	3,098	...		...	..
Endowments ..		3,780	...	...	...	2,190	...	910	...	680	...	...	...	..
Other sources.	...	31	...	...	...	...	...	...	...	30	...	1	...	...

XXVIII.—Hospitals and Dispensaries in 1912.

Name of hospital or dispensary.	Whether Government, Local Fund, Municipal or private.	In-patients. Number of beds available for. Men.	Women.	In-patients. Daily average number treated. Men.	Women.	Children.	Total.	Out-patients. Average daily attendance. Men.	Women.	Children.	Total.	Total number of patients treated both in-door and out-door.	Total expenditure during the year.
(1)	(2)	(3)	(4)	(5)	(6)	(7)	(8)	(9)	(10)	(11)	(12)	(13)	(14)
													RS.
Ambāsamudram	Local Fund..	5	3	5·48	1·24	0·15	6·87	61·87	27·27	39·09	128·28	18,955	3,442
Ettiyūpuram	Do. ...	...	..	...	...	...	...	39·08	14·60	22·49	76·17	8,944	1,853
Kāyalpatnam	Do. ...	...	...	...	...	...	...	42·18	30·88	36·21	109·27	12,830	2,150
Kōilpatti	Do. ...	...	...	...	...	...	...	32·28	15·85	13·67	61·80	10,249	1,859
Kulasēkarapatnam	Do. ...	...	..	...	..	...	...	28·23	17·34	18·13	63·70	6,529	1,802
Mēlappālaiyam	Municipal ...	...	...	...	...	...	..	34·63	17·87	17·59	70·09	11,022	1,215
Mēlavīrarāghavapuram	Do. ...	...	...	...	...	.	...	41·28	14·07	20·08	75·43	12,188	1,973
Nānguneri	Local Fund...	4	2	1·89	0·11	...	1·50	37·02	16·75	21·28	75·05	11,821	8,277
Ottappidāram	Do. ...	2	2	0·49	0·05	0·01	0·55	16·68	8·11	10·28	35·07	6,004	1,547
Palamcottah	Municipal	33	14	22·40	4·77	1·17	28·34	90·49	31·74	36·78	159·01	24,510	11,060
Panakudi	Local Fund...		...	...	...	...	.	23·50	7·95	9·81	41·26	7,848	1,044
Sankaranainārkōil	Do. ..	2	2	2·76	0·32	.	3·08	32·29	10·54	17·65	60·48	10,953	1,786
Sōranādēvi	Do. ..	...	...	...	...	...	..	40·98	18·86	18·42	78·26	14,348	2,226
Sivagiri	Do. ..	...	...	...	...	...	...	27·54	9·88	15·95	53·37	8,440	1,499
Srīvaikuntam	Do. ...	4	2	1·87	0·36	0·04	2·27	52·10	24·08	28·01	99·19	20,290	2,820
Tenkāsi	Do. ...	...	...	...	...	...	..	60·47	29·50	34·91	124·88	15,251	2,340
Tinnevelly	Do. ...	8	4	5·93	2·40	0·22	8·55	86·80	25·07	33·40	145·27	19,643	4,456
Tinnevelly Branch (Pēttai) ...	Do. ...	..	...	..	...	...	...	20·02	7·76	11·13	38·91	6,497	1,709

XXVIII.—Hospitals and Dispensaries in 1912—*cont.*

Name of hospital or dispensary.	Whether Government, Local Fund, Municipal or private.	In-patients. Number of beds available for. Men.	Women.	Daily average number treated. Men.	Women.	Chil-dren.	Total.	Out-patients. Average daily attendance. Men.	Women.	Chil-dren.	Total.	Total number of patients treated both in-door and out-door.	Total expenditure during the year.
(1)	(2)	(8)	(4)	(5)	(6)	(7)	(8)	(9)	(10)	(11)	(12)	(13)	(14)
													RS.
Tiruchendūr	Local Fund...	...	...	...	...	...	...	30·66	16·44	18·55	65·65	8,091	1,775
Tirukkarunkudi	Do. ...	...	...	...	...	...	...	16·56	7·20	8·75	32·51	4,855	1,195
Tuticorin	Municipal ...	30	25	16·49	12·55	0·69	29·73	102·19	48·92	56·44	207·55	20,101	8,335
Vīrakēralampudūr	Local Fund...	...	...	...	...	...	...	24·40	9·00	11·88	45·28	8,588	1,104
Christianagaram	Mission ...	...	..	...	...	...	...	34·22	13·07	12·36	59·65	7,008	897
Idayankudi	Do. ...	...	...	...	...	...	...	19·20	8·21	9·32	36·73	7,042	695
Pndiyamputtūr	Do. ...	...	...	...	..	...	...	12·80	6·20	9·00	28·00	2,393	782
Nāgalāpuram	Do. ..	...	...	...	...	.	...	13·80	6·87	7·78	28·40	8,962	1,257
Nāzareth	Do. ...	10	10	12·08	3·22	1·55	16·85	61·09	32·52	60·78	154·39	16,324	2,274
Sawyerpuram	Do. ...	4	4	0·63	0·20	0·19	1·02	21·55	15·46	12·01	49·02	7,129	999
Puducōttah Arunāchala's Edward Dispensary.	Private ...	...	...	...	...	...	...	10·10	6·40	4·20	20·70	7,576	776
Palamcottah (Women and Children's Hospital).	Local Fund ..	...	4	...	2·83	0·10	2·93	...	48·82	23·51	72·33	13,106	4,004
Sāttānkulam	Do. ...	...	...	...	...	...	...	29·89	16·21	14·57	60·17	3,186	1,090
	Total ...	102	72	69·52	28·05	4·12	101·69	1,148·40	558·44	648·98	2,350·82	848,673	72,740

XXIX.—Vaccination.

Local Fund Circles and Municipalities.	Number of persons successfully vaccinated.			Registered birth-rate per 1,000 of population in			Average number of successful cases of vaccination on children under one year during the three years ending 1912-13.
	1910–11.	1911–12.	1912–13.	1910.	1911.	1912.	
(1)	(2)	(3)	(4)	(5)	(6)	(7)	(8)
Circles.							
Sermādevi	17,357	22,258	20,090	34·4	32·3	31·8	10,559
Srivaikuntam ..	18,749	19,388	21,157				10,486
Koilpatti	14,383	15,409	17,550				7,522
Municipalities.							
Tinnevelly ...	1,430	1,767	1,871	38·0	35·1	36·2	1,148
Palamcottah ...	1,584	1,616	1,671	42·5	36·4	37·5	920
Tuticorin .	2,643	3,776	1,671	28·3	28·3	34·5	997
District Total ...	56,146	64,214	64,010	34·6	32·3	31·6	31,632

Note.—Figures for Revenue taluks are not separately available.

XXX.—Civil Justice.

(Average of the statistics for the three years 1910—12.)

Class of Courts.	Number of all original suits disposed of.	Average value of suits of which value was estimable in money.	Number of appealable decrees passed in disposed of cases.	Appeals preferred.	Appeals decided.	Decisions confirmed.	Percentage of decisions confirmed to total disposals.
(1)	(2)	(3)	(4)	(5)	(6)	(7)	(8)
		RS.					
Village Courts ...	10,128	...	...	...	...	...	...
Revenue Courts ...	1,811	35	115	109	221	190	86
District Munsifs' Courts	11,543	108	2,454	387	454	280	62
Subordinate Judges' Courts ...	5,116	1,826	86	28	29	16	55
District Judge's Court	2	1,548	2	...		...	...

Note.—The exclusion of the figures previous to 1910 in this table has been necessitated by the redistribution of the administrative areas of the district effected in 1910.

XXXI.—Criminal Justice.

(Number of persons convicted of certain offences in each of the three years 1910—12.)

Offence. (1)	1910. (2)	1911. (3)	1912. (4)
Murder	23	4	15
Culpable homicide	12	2	...
Hurts and assaults	141	262	265
Other offences against the person	26	15	21
Dacoity	...	.	...
Robbery	22	26	43
House-breaking	2	...	11
Cattle theft	16	34	22
Other theft	289	291	274
Other offences against property	209	193	194
Offences against public tranquillity (Chapter VIII)	203	154	72
Other offences against the Penal Code	275	298	327
Total .	1,218	1,279	1,244
Security for keeping the peace and for good behaviour	105	140	163
Offences under Madras Salt Act (IV of 1889) ...	2	...	..
Offences under Madras Abkāri Act (I of 1886) ...	1,295	1,608	1,167
Offences under Madras Forest Act (V of 1882) ...	214	407	516
Offences under Madras District Municipalities Act (IV of 1884)	620	706	945
Other offences against Special and Local laws ...	4,350	4,054	4,274
Grand Total ...	7,793	8,194	8,309

NOTE.—The omission from this table of the figures of the years previous to 1910 has been necessitated by the redistribution of administrative areas of the district effected in 1910.

XXXII.—Work of Criminal Courts.

(Average of the statistics for the three years 1910—12.)

Class of Courts. (1)	Number of original cases instituted. (2)	Number of appeals received. (3)
Village Magistrates	1,882	..
Bench do.	3,037	...
Special do.	526	...
Stipendiary Subordinate Magistrates	5,903	...
Deputy, Assistant and Joint Magistrates	335	30
District Magistrate	2	21
Court of Sessions	102	67

NOTE.—The exclusion from the table of the figures previous to 1910 has been necessitated by the reconstitution of the district effected in 1910.

XXXIII.—Police and Jails in 1912.

Taluks.	Number of Police		Police Force.						Number of known depredators.	Number of Sub-Jails.	Total accommodation in them.
	Stations.	Outposts.	Inspectors.	Sub-Inspectors.	Head Constables.	Constables.	Police Talaiyaries.	Revenue Talaiyaries.			
(1)	(2)	(3)	(4)	(5)	(6)	(7)	(8)	(9)	(10)	(11)	(12)
Sermādēvi Division.											
Nānguneri ...	5	5	1	5	15	136	...	165	455	2	24
Ambāsamudram. } **Tinnevelly Division.** Tenkāsi ... }	6	3	1	7	16	131	...	304	337	2	45
Tinnevelly ...	5	4	1	7	23	184	...	160	336	1	34
Tuticorin Division.											
Srīvaikuntam ... } Tiruchendūr ... }	7	3	1	7	16	122	...	[illegible]86	276	3	36
Kōilpatti Division.											
Kōilpatti ..	9	...	2	11	23	1[illegible]1	..	3[illegible]8	393	3	74
Sankaranainār-kōil	5	1	1	5	11	82	...	185	200	1	18
District Total ...	37	16	17*	51*	133*	1,096*	...	1,413	1,997	12	231

NOTE.—* The totals include the Reserve Force of 8 Sergeants and 2 Inspectors and 9 Sub-Inspectors (of the vacancy Reserve and readers to the District and Assistant Superintendent of Police) and the Reserve Force of 29 Head Constables and 260 Constables for the district. There is a district jail at Palamcottah with accommodation for 437 prisoners.